Columbia University

Contributions to Education

Teachers College Series

No. 896

AMS PRESS
NEW YORK

BEHAVIOR CHANGES
resulting from
A Study of Communicable Diseases

AN EVALUATION OF THE EFFECTS OF LEARNING
ON CERTAIN ACTIONS OF HIGH SCHOOL PUPILS

By JOHN URBAN

SUBMITTED IN PARTIAL FULFILLMENT OF THE REQUIREMENTS
FOR THE DEGREE OF DOCTOR OF PHILOSOPHY IN THE
FACULTY OF PHILOSOPHY, COLUMBIA UNIVERSITY

*Published with the Approval of
Professor Samuel Ralph Powers, Sponsor*

BUREAU OF PUBLICATIONS
Teachers College, Columbia University
NEW YORK · 1943

Library of Congress Cataloging in Publication Data

Urban, John, 1909-
    Behavior changes resulting from a study of communicable
diseases.

    Reprint of the 1943 ed., issued in series: Teachers
College, Columbia University. Contributions to educa-
tion, no. 896.
    Originally presented as the author's thesis, Columbia.
    Bibliography: p.
    1. Learning, Psychology of. 2. Communicable dis-
eases--Study and teaching. I. Title. II. Series:
Columbia University. Teachers College. Contributions
to education, no. 896.
LB1051.U7 1972   613'.0433   75-177687
ISBN 0-404-55896-8

From the edition of 1943, New York
First AMS edition published in 1972
Manufactured in the United States

AMS PRESS, INC.
NEW YORK, N. Y.   10003

ACKNOWLEDGMENTS

THE AUTHOR welcomes this opportunity to express his gratitude to the many persons who have given so generously of their time and talents to make this study possible.

He is particularly indebted to Professor S. Ralph Powers, in whose classes he found the inspiration for the investigation.

Professor Frederick L. Fitzpatrick acted as the author's adviser for the study, contributing much that was most stimulating and helpful. Without his interest and assistance the study would not have been possible.

Professors Irving Lorge and Helen M. Walker were more than helpful with the statistical aspects of the study. Anita D. Laton and Professor Arthur T. Jersild helped to shape the learning materials.

The author is obligated also to Leona Baumgartner, M.D., Thomas C. Davis, M.D., and D. W. Teller, M.D., for their work in validating the tests and the lists of behaviors. In this they cooperated with Professor Jean Broadhurst, Miss Charlotte M. Brothers, R. N., and Mrs. Audrey Klink Bosch. Mrs. Bosch also read carefully the learning materials and made several valuable suggestions.

Thanks are due Mrs. Lucy Rosser Herberick, Mrs. Jean Crockett Barr, Miss Marie Margot, and Dr. Herman Ward for permission to carry on observations in their English classes.

To his wife, Helen Smrha Urban, the author is most indebted for her assistance in many parts of the study.

J. U.

CONTENTS

Contents

BEHAVIOR CHANGES RESULTING FROM A STUDY OF COMMUNICABLE DISEASES

Chapter I

INTRODUCTION

EDUCATION in the United States is passing through an evolutionary period. Technological advancement, the shift of population from rural to urban centers, ideological revolutions, economic changes, and international disturbances are all leaving their impressions on our schools. We are seeing the effect of their impacts in changed educational aims, in broadened curricula, and in the theory and practice of teaching.

Half a century ago only a small percentage of the eligible population was enrolled in the secondary schools. Those who were in attendance were preparing to go to college. The primary purpose of the high school was preparation for further study. Today this has changed. Many pupils do not intend to continue their education formally. Many are in school only because attendance laws compel them to be there; others, because they are ineligible for gainful employment; still others attend because it has become the customary thing to do. Enrollments have soared. As public institutions, high schools are not selective, so that each contains a student body heterogeneous in such important aspects of life as economic level, educational background of parents, national origin, religious belief, and future educational and vocational intentions, as well as levels of achievement and ability.

This heterogeneity has complicated general education. Teachers and administrators alike have come to recognize that public schools must do more than prepare students for college, and that the aims of education must be changed. A step in this direction was taken when the Commission on the Reorganization of Secondary Education stated that "The main objectives of education are: (1) health, (2) command of the fundamental

1

processes, (3) worthy home membership, (4) vocation, (5) citizenship, (6) worthy use of leisure, and (7) ethical character."[1]

These aims of education have been modified somewhat. The Committee on the Teaching of Science, of the National Society for the Study of Education, stated that "an aim of education that seems consistent with the postulations of modern philosophy is, Life enrichment through participation in a democratic social order."[2] The implication here seems to be that general education should concern itself with those aims which, when developed through practice in a learning situation, will result in effective and desirable citizenship consistent with the traditions of our nation.

More recently this point of view has been restated. The Committee on the Function of Science in General Education, of the Progressive Education Association, believes that the "purpose of general education is to meet the needs of individuals in the basic aspects of living in such a way as to promote the fullest possible realization of personal potentialities and the most effective participation in a democratic society."[3]

With the aims of education thus undergoing changes, classroom procedures, too, have been altered. The learner is being given more individual attention; his needs are being studied more closely. Curricula have been enlarged and have come to include many non-academic subjects, to provide needed training for the pupil whose formal education will cease when he leaves the high school. New outcomes are being sought. Once the attention of both learner and teacher was focused on the acquisition of information; at that time evaluation consisted of the application of techniques intended to measure the extent of such acquisition. But as the emphasis in educational values shifted from traditional subject matter to the develop-

---

[1] *Cardinal Principles of Secondary Education*, U. S. Bureau of Secondary Education Bulletin, 1918, No. 35, pp. 10–11.

[2] National Society for the Study of Education, *Thirty-first Year Book*, Part I, "A Program for Teaching Science," p. 43.

[3] *Science in General Education*, Report of a Committee on the Function of Science in General Education, p. 23. D. Appleton-Century, New York, 1937.

ment of traits and characteristics considered desirable for meeting the needs of the individual in "the basic aspects of living," the necessity of developing techniques for evaluating the newly sought outcomes arose concurrently. Measurement of gains in information is now considered but one phase of the total evaluation of a learner's progress; much attention is being given to appraisal of changes in ways of thinking, in specific feelings, attitudes, and interests, in "ways of looking at life," and in overt behavior.

This investigation is centered on the problem of studying changes in overt behavior resulting from situations set up in the classroom. The need for such a study has been indicated in the published and unpublished works of the Bureau of Educational Research in Science, of Teachers College, Columbia University, and elsewhere. The Committee Appointed to Consider a Proposal for an Enlarged Program of Work in the Field of General Education at Teachers College (Columbia University) recommended that teaching units be set up and taught, and that "each teacher should try to achieve some idea of the following changes occurring in his students . . . changes in overt behavior."[4] Later, in the same report, it is stated that "throughout our entire work attention must be centered upon overt behavior as evidence that the traits and capacities acquired by the individual are in fact influencing his behavior."[5]

Some significance may perhaps be attached to the fact that each of the several sets of "Suggestions for Teaching," prepared under the auspices of the Bureau of Educational Research in Science, suggests that changes in overt behavior be evaluated, but none of them gives specific procedures. For example, Laton and Pilley[6] say that "evaluation should be aimed at discovering to what extent teaching has brought about in students changes in behavior." In the unit entitled "Genetics" it is recom-

---

[4] Report of a Committee Appointed to Consider a Proposal for an Enlarged Program of Work in the Field of General Education at Teachers College, Columbia University, p. 46. Unpublished, 1938.   [5] *Ibid.,* p. 51.

[6] Laton, Anita D. and Pilley, J. G., *Source Unit on Scientific Method,* p. 52. Bureau of Publications, Teachers College, Columbia University, 1938. (Mimeographed.)

mended that behaviors be observed to determine changes. The unit on "Life Span," by Laton[7] and others, goes a step further, for it contains some ideas on evaluation of changes in overt behavior, such as "feeding children correctly, arranging daily routine for children," and then continues "observation of overt behavior depends upon opportunities available."

In his unit on "Physiological Exchanges of Materials and Energy," Manwell[8] proposes that "students record choices of foods made by fellow students in the school cafeteria." He also suggests the use of questionnaires on proper care of the skin and hair, and interviews and records of casual conversations regarding patent medicines, as ways of gathering evidence of changes in overt behaviors.

Thus it may be seen that while ideas on changes in overt behavior are being evaluated, none of those mentioned are sufficiently specific to indicate clearly what may be done.

The area of "Communicable Diseases" was chosen as the stage for this investigation for a number of reasons. Educators have for many years recognized that the attainment and maintenance of good health is a primary aim of education. Health is listed as the first of the Seven Cardinal Principles of Education. Provision has been made in the curriculum for opportunity to study the problems of health. Courses in physiology and hygiene have attempted to deal specifically with this topic, and most high school biology courses devote attention to it. The Report of the Committee on the Function of Science of the Progressive Education Association has stated that "in meeting the needs of adolescents in the basic life aspect of personal living, the need for health is recognized," and that "detailed knowledge about how to prevent different kinds of infections is necessary of course, and to some large degree will vary with the diseases present in the locality. Certain diseases are so widely spread that a detailed knowledge of their etiology, and prevention, is necessary for all adolescents."

[7] Laton, Anita D. and others, *Source Unit on "Life Span,"* p. 28. Bureau of Publications, Teachers College, Columbia University, 1938. (Mimeographed.)

[8] Manwell, E. A., *Physiological Exchanges of Materials and Energy,* p. 64. Bureau of Publications, Teachers College, Columbia University, 1938. (Mimeo.)

Despite improved methods for controlling communicable diseases, they still persist as important personal, family, and national problems. Except for typhoid fever, diphtheria, and smallpox, there has been no general decline in the number of cases per 1,000 population, according to the statistics of the United States Public Health Service. Table I illustrates this point by showing the rates per 1,000 population of our commonest reportable communicable diseases for the years 1922–1924 and those of 1937–1939.

TABLE I

THE INCIDENCE RATES PER 1,000 POPULATION OF SOME COMMON
REPORTABLE COMMUNICABLE DISEASES IN 1922–1924
AND 1937–1939*

Disease	1922	1923	1924	1937	1938	1939
Chicken pox	1.22	1.41	1.81	2.175	2.203	1.984
Diphtheria	1.59	1.31	1.07	0.221	0.234	0.185
Gonorrhea	...	...	...	1.556	1.396	1.364
Influenza	3.66	4.66	...	4.683	1.588	2.706
Malaria	...	...	...	0.940	0.702	0.656
Measles	2.55	7.72	4.58	2.487	6.319	3.094
Mumps	0.51	0.57	1.28	1.400	1.408	1.319
Pneumonia	...	...	...	1.640	1.573	1.352
Scarlet fever	1.50	1.56	1.66	1.771	1.456	1.249
Smallpox	0.31	0.28	0.35	0.090	0.115	0.076
Syphilis	...	...	...	3.297	3.661	3.709
Tuberculosis	...	...	...		0.899	0.890
Typhoid	0.34	0.32	0.33	0.124	0.114	0.100
Whooping cough	1.08	1.61	1.47	1.661	1.746	1.405

* Adapted from *"The Notifiable Diseases, Prevalence in States,"* Reprints No. 879 (1922), No. 974 (1923), No. 1056 (1924) from the Public Health Reports, U. S. Public Health Service, Government Printing Office, Washington, D. C., and from *"The Notifiable Diseases, Prevalence in States,"* Supplements No. 147 (1937), No. 160 (1938), No. 163 (1939), to the Public Health Reports, Public Health Service, Government Printing Office, Washington, D. C.

It must be recognized that while the statistics submitted in Table I indicate the general trend, they are not so reliable as might be assumed. Some of the increase in the rates of prevalence quoted for the later years may be due to improved methods of reporting. It will be noted that no figures are given for gonorrhea, malaria, pneumonia, syphilis, and tuberculosis for the 1922–1924 period. This is apparently because no statistics were compiled by the United States Public Health Service during that time for these diseases. Laws dealing with the reporting of diseases vary considerably from state to state. The rates cited are probably underestimates, for it is safe to assume that many cases of communicable diseases are never brought to the attention of a physician, or never reported by the physician to the state or local board of health.

Then, too, some of the diseases become epidemic in a cycle of years. For example, the reduction of the influenza rate from 4.683 in 1937 to 1.588 in 1938 was not due to the development of new methods of control; it was due to the fact that in the former year the incidence was of epidemic proportions which had dwindled considerably by the end of the next year. The rates for both syphilis and gonorrhea may be considered too low, in all probability, since it is known that many individuals suffering from these diseases often do not consult a physician.

Another reason for selecting this area for the proposed study is that there are a number of directly observable behaviors with implications for control of communicable diseases; these are of such nature that they are related closely to the learning materials offered to the pupil, and some of the changes which occur may be seen at first hand. In other words, at least some of the desirable changes may be seen and studied directly. This is important. In much educational research considerable evidence is gathered by means of paper and pencil tests. These are at best at least one step removed from the actual desired outcome: the practice and application of principles learned in the class situation. Such tests are likely to prove that the learner knows what he should do; however, whether or not this knowledge is translated into changes in overt behavior is problematical. For example, most persons know that when they have a cold they should remain at home, resting in bed. A moment's reflection is sufficient to bring the realization that many persons having such knowledge do not act accordingly.

Not all of the changes proposed for study can be observed directly. It is therefore necessary to resort to the techniques of the interview to obtain some items of information. It is obviously impossible for the investigator to spend sufficient time with pupils involved in the study to gain a complete picture of what they do outside the classroom by watching them, and for that reason it is necessary to depend upon their testimony.

The question may be asked: Why was the area limited to the communicable diseases? To this question there are several answers. Students have had less intimate experience with the other kinds of diseases, such as the various heart ailments, cancer, and so on. Materials on these latter conditions are not as available on the high school level. Furthermore, there is probably less opportunity for the study of changes in behavior in connection with them. Finally, health is but one unit in a course in general biology intended primarily for ninth year pupils; to include everything which could be included would extend the time necessary for study of the unit to an extent that would unbalance the year's work, and leave other aims unfulfilled. Diseases caused by deficient nutrition were studied separately in a unit on that topic.

The following summary recapitulates the points thus far made. (1) Education is changing its aims, shifting from emphasis on preparing for college to preparation for citizenship in a democracy. (2) With the changes in goals, new techniques are needed for evaluating outcomes, and for determining whether or not the outcomes are being achieved. (3) It is the purpose of this investigation to study the changes in overt behavior of high school pupils who have studied a unit on communicable diseases.

Chapter II

THE INVESTIGATION

STATEMENT OF THE PROBLEM

THE PROBLEM on which this investigation proposes to throw light may be stated thus: Can the study of communicable diseases by high school general biology pupils result in desirable changes in the overt behavior related to the control of these diseases? Does the acquisition of information have an effect on what the learner does, or does it remain purely an intellectual experience? Solution of the problem will be attempted by determining whether or not the outcomes sought are actually achieved. If in some instances the results seem significant, and if in others they do not, an attempt will be made to interpret the factors involved in the experiment which may explain such variations.

As used in this investigation, the term "overt behavior" refers only to those actions by the learner which have a direct function in the communicability of the diseases studied. Desirable behavior is that which is recognized as being of value in avoiding infection, or that which minimizes the possibility of infecting others. Behavior is considered undesirable if it may possibly result in the contraction of a communicable disease, or if it may result in the spread of infection to others.

SELECTION OF DISEASES FOR STUDY

Diseases to be studied were selected by a procedure similar to that used by Laton.[1] Reports of the United States Public Health Service[2] covering the years 1916–1939, inclusive, were

[1] Laton, Anita D., *The Psychology of Learning Applied to Health Education Through Biology*, pp. 9–15.
[2] A complete list of these is given in the Bibliography on pages 94–96.

studied to determine which diseases were most prevalent in the United States. A list of the commonest communicable diseases was then compiled on the basis of rates of prevalence. It was interesting to find that this list of fifteen diseases was very much like that used in Laton's study, with the exception of rabies and yellow fever, included by Laton, but replaced by syphilis and gonorrhea in this investigation. The list of diseases selected as having greatest value for study in this investigation includes the following:

chicken pox	malaria	smallpox
colds	measles	syphilis
diphtheria	mumps	tuberculosis
gonorrhea	pneumonia	typhoid fever
influeneza	scarlet fever	whooping cough

Diphtheria, smallpox, and typhoid fever are not so prevalent as some of the others; their incidence has been declining. But these diseases must be constantly fought, for if they are neglected they may easily become common again. For that reason they were included in this study.

SELECTION OF BEHAVIORS FOR STUDY

The list of behaviors to be considered in the investigation was determined from a preliminary survey made during 1939–1940. One hundred and ten students in four biology classes were observed and interviewed to determine whether changes in behavior needed to be made a goal of instruction; it was also determined specifically what kinds of changes were desirable. This preliminary survey led to the conclusion that pupils have a number of undesirable behavior traits which need to be changed.

Observation of pupil behavior in the classroom showed that the following actions were common:

1. Pupils very frequently put one or more fingers in their mouth, or gnawed at their knuckles, or put the side of their hand in their mouth.

2. Other objects, such as coins, pencils, pens, paper clips, paper, beads, bracelets, combs, small mirrors, erasers, rubber bands, marbles, coat lapels, neckties, handkerchiefs, etc., were often put into the mouth.
3. Biting of fingernails was often observed.
4. It was not uncommon for pupils to insert a finger into one of the nostrils.
5. Pupils frequently rubbed their eyes with their fingers.
6. Handkerchiefs were almost never used when pupils coughed.
7. Handkerchiefs were almost never used when pupils sneezed.

By interviews with all pupils it was learned that their behavior in situations outside the classroom also needed changing. These interviews disclosed that:

1. Very few pupils washed their hands before eating lunch in the school cafeteria or other places away from home.
2. Many pupils did not regularly wash their hands before having dinner at home.
3. A large percentage of the pupils did not wash their hands after being to the toilet at school, at home, or other places.
4. Pupils frequently "took a bite" of food already partly eaten by another person, or shared with others the food they were eating. Such food included candy, cake, ice cream, and fruit in most cases.
5. Some pupils shared towels and washcloths with other members of their families, or with the whole family.
6. Most pupils used drinking glasses in common with other members of the family.
7. Many pupils were negligent about having a clean handkerchief each day.

Interviews with pupils who had been absent from school because of communicable illness revealed that:

1. Many continued to attend school even after the symptoms of their illness had appeared.

2. When ill pupils did remain home from school, they often did not go to bed immediately, or remain in bed, but were likely to try to carry on some activity in which they were interested.

3. Ill pupils did not remain in bed until they had recovered from their sickness, but came back to school or went to other places while still suffering from their illness.

4. When pupils remained home because of illness their pulse rate was not taken, nor in most cases was their temperature taken.

5. A physician was seldom consulted even though the child had been ill for several days.

6. Sick children quite commonly had a number of visitors.

7. A large variety of parent-prescribed patent medicines were used to treat the illness.

8. In most cases, no particular precautions were taken in the home to prevent the spread of the infection by means of eating utensils.

9. In most instances no special precautions were taken about the possible spread of infection through such agencies as handkerchiefs, towels, washcloths, etc., used by the ill pupil.

These observations and interviews disclosed the need for changes in behavior. They were made the basis for the investigation. To make sure that the list of behaviors thus determined was a valid one in view of the objectives of this study, it was submitted to a group of persons who may be deemed to have some competence in the area. Two of the group were practicing physicians, two were high school biology teachers, one was the school nurse, and one was a member of the Bureau of Educational Research in Science. No item was included in the list of behaviors to be studied unless it was judged important by at least four of these experts.

As a further check on the validity of the list an authoritative published source was consulted. This was the United States Public Health Service Reprint No. 1697, entitled "The Control of Communicable Diseases."[3] For example, in its section on influenza the committee which prepared the report recommends that "Kissing, the use of common towels, glasses, eating utensils or toilet articles should be avoided."[4] It is also recommended that "to minimize the severity of the disease and to protect the patient from secondary infections and thus reduce mortality, the patient should go to bed at the beginning of an attack and not return to work without the approval of the physician."[5] For measles it is recommended that methods of concurrent disinfection be applied to "all articles soiled with secretions from the nose and throat."[6] In the section on whooping cough "education in habits of personal cleanliness"[7] is recommended. This is defined as "keeping the body clean by sufficiently frequent soap and water baths, washing hands in soap and water after voiding bowels and bladder and always before eating; keeping hands and unclean articles, or articles which have been used for toilet purposes by others, away from nose, mouth, eyes, ears, and genitalia; avoiding the use of common or unclean eating, drinking, or toilet articles of any kind, such as towels, handkerchiefs, drinking cups, hairbrushes, pipes, etc.; avoiding close exposure of persons to spray from the nose and mouth, as in coughing, sneezing, laughing or talking."[8]

The preliminary study, therefore, indicated that the high school biology pupil needs experiences which will lead him to change his overt behavior with respect to these relationships of communicable diseases. Consultation with the list of competent persons and reference to the authoritative source previously mentioned validated this list of needed changes.

Certain basic considerations seemed essential in undertaking the investigation. These were:

---

[3] The Control of Communicable Diseases," by Haven Emerson, M.D., and others comprising a Subcommittee on Communicable Disease Control, of the Committee on Research and Standards of the American Public Health Association, 1936. Published as Reprint No. 1697, from the Public Health Reports, Vol. 50, No. 32, August 9, 1935, pp. 1017–1077. Government Printing Office, Washington, D. C.

[4] *Ibid.,* p. 20.   [5] *Ibid.,* p. 20.

[6] *Ibid.,* p. 23.   [7] *Ibid.,* p. 47.

[8] *Ibid.,* pp. 3–4.

1. Learning should result in the achievement of outcomes recognized as being of value.
2. One outcome of learning should be a change in behavior from undesirable to desirable, such changes to be the product of the learner's recognition of the factors involved in determining. such desirability and undesirability. Parallel with the change from undesirable to desirable behavior should be the development of new actions not previously used by the learner.
3. Pupils in high school biology classes perform a number of actions which may be considered undesirable.
4. Because man's physical welfare is properly the concern of the learner in biology classes, and because communicable diseases have important effects on the learner and on the society in which he lives, a unit of learning materials on this topic may be included in the course and instruction should be pointed in the direction of bringing about desirable changes in behavior.

STEPS IN PROCEDURE

The following brief outline summarizes the procedure followed in the investigation:

1. A preliminary study was made to determine the character and extent of pupil behavior considered undesirable from the standpoint of communicability of diseases. The data obtained were so very similar to those obtained in the actual investigation that they are not reported. Study of the chapter on "Data of the Experiment" will give a true picture of what was found in the preliminary study as well as in the investigation.
2. The educational implications of our knowledge concerning the communicable diseases were explored and summarized.[9]
3. On the basis of the exploration of the area, and with the

---

[9] Richter, Marion; Urban, John; and Fitzpatrick, F. L., *The Educational Implications of Our Knowledge Concerning Communicable Diseases.* (Unpub.)

desired changes in behavior in mind, learning materials were selected and organized for use by the pupils.

4. An achievement test, in two comparable forms, was constructed. Form A was used as a pre-test and retention test; Form B was used to measure learning at the conclusion of pupil study of the unit.

5. Student behavior was determined by observations and interviews before the learning materials were studied.

6. Two classes, used as controls, studied a unit of work not closely related to communicable diseases; two experimental classes studied the unit prepared for the experiment.

7. Observations and interviews were repeated at the close of the teaching of the experimental unit; this was done in both the control and the experimental classes, to determine what changes had occurred.

8. Twelve weeks after the experimental group had completed its study of the unit, the observations and interviews were repeated to determine whether or not the changes in behavior showed tendencies of becoming permanent changes.

9. The changes found were then analyzed to discover:
   a. The nature of the changes.
   b. The extent of the changes.
   c. The relationships between changes and various educational factors.

THE EXPERIMENTAL SITUATION

The experiment was undertaken in the Millburn Township Public High School, in Millburn, New Jersey. This is a six-year unit, including grades seven to twelve, enrolling approximately one thousand pupils of both sexes. The community is typically suburban; many of its citizens commute daily to metropolitan centers where they hold positions in business and in the professions. Economically, the general level of the community is above average; a great many parents of pupils in the school have college degrees, and about 60 per cent of the members of the graduating class normally enroll in colleges. Practically all the residents of the township are of the white race. There are many of foreign extraction, but the majority of pupils come from families whose members have been citizens of this country for two or three generations or more.

Government of the township is by a committee of citizens; the population is about twelve thousand. A board of health performs the functions usually assigned to such a group.

One hundred and twenty-six pupils were included in the investigation; this number comprised all pupils in four classes except two, who were omitted from consideration because of very irregular attendance. Pupils were of mixed age, intelligence quotient, achievement, and background, but the experimental group and the control group were fundamentally similar, as is shown in Chapter VI. They were from college preparatory, general, and commercial courses.

Practically all students in both groups had had a semester of general science in the seventh grade and another semester in the eighth grade. A few had also had a year of general science in the ninth year.

Both groups had studied the same materials in their biology work up to the time of the experiment. The unit on communicable diseases had been preceded by a unit on human anatomy, physiology, and nutrition. While the experimental group was studying communicable diseases the control group was considering "Green Plants and Their Relation to Man."

Six weeks were allowed for the study of the experimental unit, including the time needed for the two information tests. The net length of each period was fifty minutes. Facilities for laboratory work, for visual education, and for pupil research were quite good. A number of different biology textbooks were available in multiple copies; reference books could be had in the library; lantern slides, motion pictures, and film strips were used. A microprojector, opaque projector, and microscopes were used. Equipment in the laboratory included a bacteriological incubator, an Arnold sterilizer, petri dishes, nutrient media, and other articles.

Chapter III

ORGANIZATION OF EDUCATIONAL EXPERIENCES

DEFINITION OF THE LEARNER'S NEEDS

EDUCATIONAL materials and experiences for the experimental group were selected on the basis of the needs of the individual. The needs in this instance have been indicated in Chapters I and II. They may be re-emphasized here.

Communicable diseases are a persistent human problem. Every child of adolescent age has experienced one or more of them. Illness of this nature often has a profound physiological and psychological effect on the individual. It may have an important influence on the financial status of the family; its cost is often considerable. Widespread prevalence of contagion and infection reduces the working power of the nation and saps its vitality. Some of the diseases have a direct effect upon the birth rate and population growth.

Communicable diseases are caused by pathogens which are found everywhere. All people are susceptible to diseases, and so should be aware of their danger in order to avoid them. Every individual can take certain simple precautions against them. If a disease is contracted by an individual or by one of his family, certain further precautions are necessary to prevent its spread. These steps are based on knowledge of the characteristics of the particular disease involved. Intelligent action depends upon well-established scientific information.

Good health is one of the leading assets of any nation. As such, it must be conserved. Its conservation, in a democratic social order, becomes the responsibility of every citizen. Cooperation in maintaining home and community sanitation is

16

necessary. Such cooperation, based on accurate information, can result in improved conditions from which all benefit. In brief, the establishment and maintenance of good health is both an individual and a sociological problem. Since society is composed of individuals, education must furnish experiences which will result in learning which will bring about desirable changes in behavior.

Having stated that communicable diseases are of importance to the learner, consideration may be given to an exploration of the area. The substance of it is given in the following out-line, which summarizes fundamental facts derived from many recent sources. The interest and needs of the learner, socio-logical implications, and appropriateness for use at the ninth grade level were kept in mind when the selection and organ-ization were done.

Major Generalizations and Supporting Ideas

I. The control of communicable diseases is a problem of im-portance to the nation, the family, and the individual.
  1. Sickness is an important factor in determining the national welfare.
    a. Communicable diseases reduce the ability of a nation to produce goods and materials.
    b. The military strength of a nation is reduced by diseases known to be communicable.
    c. Large numbers of physically and mentally handicapped individuals whose inability to care for themselves is due to disease must be supported by various governmental agencies, thus increasing the tax burden of the popula-tion at large.
    d. Considerable funds are appropriated annually for the establishment and operation of facilities for the treat-ment of persons suffering from communicable diseases.
  2. Communicable diseases may have a considerable influence on the welfare of the family.
    a. Illness or death of the wage-earner in the family may seriously disrupt its economic stability.
    b. If it is the mother of the family who is ill, her incapacity may impose an emotional or psychological handicap on the children.

     c. Certain communicable diseases may interfere with normal reproductive processes, causing sterility or stillbirths, preventing the establishment of a normal family group.

3. Normal development of the adolescent depends partly on freedom from communicable diseases.
    a. Some diseases, if uncontrolled, would have a high rate of incidence with a high mortality rate, as has been shown by their past history.
    b. Some diseases affect the individual in such a way that he is hampered in physical activity for years afterward.
    c. Severe illness may retard the progress of the child in school, delaying completion of his education by one or more years.
    d. Protracted illness may have psychological complications which handicap the child afterward.

II. Communicable diseases are caused by a variety of pathogenic organisms.
1. Parasitic bacteria are responsible for many diseases.
    a. Bacteria are microscopic plants varying in size from about 1/500th of an inch to approximately 1/50,000th of an inch.
    b. It has been estimated that there may be as many as 500,000,000,000 bacteria to a gram of weight.
    c. Bacteria are found practically everywhere.
    d. Environmental conditions determine the number and kinds of bacteria found in a given place.
    e. Bacteria may be classified according to their shape in three general groups:
        (1) the rod-shaped bacilli;
        (2) the spherical cocci;
        (3) the spiral spirilla.
    f. Bacteria reproduce by simple fission.
    g. Under optimum conditions bacteria reproduce rapidly.
    h. Some pathogenic bacteria survive unfavorable environmental conditions by forming spores.
    i. Bacteria may be killed by direct sunlight, by drying the material in which they are found, by heat, by certain organic chemicals, and by compounds containing salts of the heavy metals. Ultraviolet rays are now also being used to kill bacteria.
    j. Many kinds of bacteria are either beneficial to man or neutral in their relationship to him.

2. Parasitic Protozoa are responsible for a number of communicable diseases.

   a. Protozoa are microscopic animals consisting of one cell.

   b. Protozoa are found wherever water is present, including the bodies of many metazoan organisms.

   c. Protozoa· are responsible for such communicable diseases as malaria, amoebic dysentery, African sleeping sickness, and others.

   d. Protozoa may reproduce either sexually or asexually, according to the species.

   e. Some Protozoa meet unfavorable environmental conditions by the formation of cysts.

   f. There are four classes of Protozoa, each with its distinguishing characteristics.

3. Some communicable diseases are caused by pathogens, all of whose characteristics have not yet been ascertained.

   a. Filtrable viruses cause some of the most severe and most common communicable diseases.

   b. Filtrable viruses can be cultured in living tissues, in which they exhibit the phenomena of growth and reproduction.

   c. Filtrable viruses seem to have little resistance to high temperatures or chemical action.

   d. It is the opinion of some scientists that filtrable viruses are protein molecules characterized by the properties of living things.

   e. Tissues infected by filtrable viruses sometimes show the presence of inclusion bodies in the nucleus or cytoplasm of their cells.

   f. Some plant diseases are known to be due to filtrable viruses.

4. Some communicable diseases are caused by organisms known as Spirochetes, others by Rickettsiae.

   a. Spirochetes are parasitic one-celled organisms having a spiral form.

   b. Spirochetes can move in liquids.

   c. The length of Spirochetes varies from 1/1,000th of an inch to about 4/25,000th of an inch.

   d. Syphilis is caused by Spirochetes.

   e. Rickettsiae are very small microorganisms named after the scientist Ricketts.

   f. Some Rickettsiae are rod-shaped; others are spherical.

   g. Rickettsiae are the causes of typhus and spotted fever.

III. Communicable diseases have certain attributes on the basis of which they may be recognized.

1. Each communicable disease has a specific causing agent or agents.

   a. Pathogenic bacilli are known to be the causes of diphtheria, typhoid fever, tuberculosis, and whooping cough, among other diseases.

   b. Pathogenic cocci are the causes of gonorrhea, pneumonia, and probably scarlet fever, among other diseases.

   c. Chicken pox, the common cold, influenza, measles, mumps, and smallpox are thought to be caused by filtrable viruses.

   d. Malaria is caused by parasitic Protozoans, as are amoebic dysentery and African sleeping sickness.

   e. Syphilis is caused by a Spirochete, *Treponema pallidum*.

2. Each communicable disease has certain known sources of infection.

   a. Sources of infection are places from which pathogens are spread.

   b. Discharges from the nose, mouth, throat, trachea, bronchi, and lungs are the sources of infection for some diseases.

   c. Bowel and kidney discharges are the sources of infection for some diseases.

   d. The blood of persons suffering from such diseases as malaria is a source of infection.

   e. Lesions on the skin and mucous membranes of persons suffering from certain diseases are sources of infection.

3. Disease organisms may be conveyed from one person to another in a variety of ways.

   a. Direct contact with a patient having a communicable disease may result in its conveyance to another person, as in the case of kissing, being close to an ill person when he coughs or sneezes, etc.

   b. Eating utensils, towels, toilet articles, clothes, bed linens, drinking glasses, and objects soiled by discharges from the body of an ill person may be the mode of conveyance of pathogens.

   c. Food containing pathogenic microorganisms may convey diseases. Milk, sea food, fruits, vegetables, and meats are potential conveyors.

   d. Some disease organisms are conveyed in contaminated water.

    e. Insects such as flies, fleas, mosquitoes, and lice convey disease organisms.

       (1) Some insects transmit diseases mechanically.

       (2) Some insects are intermediate hosts to pathogenic organisms.

    f. Some mammals function as reservoirs of infection, by acting as hosts to insects and arachnids which transmit the disease organisms.

    g. Some diseases are conveyed to man by mammals, or in products that come from mammals.

4. Each communicable disease has a typical though variable period of incubation.

    a. Some diseases have very short periods of incubation, lasting from twenty-four to seventy-two hours.

    b. Some periods of incubation are of longer duration, several days to several weeks.

    c. In a few diseases the period of incubation may be several months.

    d. The period of incubation is the time from exposure to a disease until the first symptoms appear.

5. The length of time during which a disease is communicable varies with the different diseases.

    a. Some diseases are communicable so long as the causative organism is present in the body of the individual.

    b. Communicability in some diseases is limited to a defined period of time during the presence of the disease in the individual.

    c. Some diseases are communicable only if transmitting agents, such as mosquitoes in the case of malaria, are present.

    d. The period of communicability for some diseases (i.e., mumps, influenza, and pneumonia) is still not well defined.

6. Individuals vary in their susceptibility to communicable diseases.

    a. Susceptibility is the tendency of a person to be lacking in resistance to a disease.

    b. Everyone is susceptible, at one time or another in his life, to some of the communicable diseases.

    c. Children are more susceptible to some diseases than are adults.

    d. Infants seem to be born with immunity to some diseases; such immunity often lasts until they are six to nine months old.

e. An attack of some of the diseases seems to confer immunity of a permanent nature to the disease in question.

f. An attack of some of the diseases seems to result in a temporary immunity to the disease in question.

g. An attack of some diseases seems to result in very little immunity.

7. Communicable diseases vary in seasonal prevalence.

   a. Some of the diseases are commonest during the winter and spring months.

   b. Some diseases seem to be equally prevalent throughout the year.

   c. Some diseases are most prevalent during the fall and winter months.

8. Communicable diseases may be recognized by their symptoms.

   a. Some communicable diseases are characterized by fever at their onset, and sometimes in their later stages as well.

   b. Abnormal amount of discharge from the nose and throat typifies some of the diseases.

   c. Coughing is a symptom of some of the diseases.

   d. Headache, aching joints, general lassitude, and ill-feeling are symptoms of some of the diseases.

   e. Skin rashes, eruptions on the skin and mucous membranes, and lesions at points of infection are indications of disease.

   f. The symptomatology of communicable diseases is complex and in the main should be left to the physician.

   g. Each disease has a number of symptoms; diagnosis of each case needs to be made on the basis of the case history; symptoms recognized by the untrained person may be misleading.

IV. The human body is provided with means for preventing infections and for combatting them if they occur.

1. Entrance of pathogens into the body is made more difficult by its protective mechanisms.

   a. The external skin is a barrier to the entrance of pathogens into the body, and, to a lesser extent, so is a mucous membrane.

   b. Scratches and breaks in the skin surface permit entry of disease microorganisms.

      c. Epithelial cells in the respiratory system remove some microorganisms by ciliary action. Hairs in the nose help purify air that is breathed in.

      d. Mucus produced by mucous membranes has a slightly germicidal effect.

      e. Elimination of mucus from the respiratory organs results in the elimination of some pathogens.

      f. Hydrochloric acid in the stomach is thought to eliminate some kinds of bacteria as agents of disease.

2. When pathogens invade the body they cause the formation by the body of substances which act against them.

      a. Antibodies, which counteract the disease organisms or their harmful products, are created by the body tissues.

         (1) Antitoxins are formed to neutralize toxins formed by pathogens.

         (2) Lysins, which have a tendency to "dissolve" pathogens, may be formed in the body.

         (3) Agglutinins and precipitins, which cause bacteria to be clumped together in the body, making them more susceptible to destruction by white corpuscles, may be formed.

         (4) Opsonins, which seem to make bacteria more digestible to white corpuscles, may also be formed.

      b. Antibodies are specific for each communicable disease.

      c. White corpuscles ingest pathogenic bacteria, thus destroying them.

V. Man has developed techniques by means of which he is able to protect himself against some of the communicable diseases.

1. Immunities to certain diseases may be artificially developed.

      a. Immunity is the ability to resist diseases.

      b. Some individuals have a natural immunity to some diseases.

      c. Individuals not immune to smallpox, diphtheria, and typhoid fever, etc., may be artificially immunized.

      d. Artificial immunity may be either passive or active.

         (1) Passive immunity results from introducing into the body of the individual antibodies produced in an animal, or in a person who has recovered from the disease.

         (2) Active immunity results from introducing into the body substances which cause it to develop its own antibodies.

  e. Immunity against one disease gives no protection against other diseases.

  f. Artificial immunity is often temporary and must be renewed to insure prolonged immunity.

  g. Whether or not a person is immune to some of the diseases may be determined by tests.

   (1) The Schick test determines whether or not one is immune to diphtheria.

   (2) The Dick test determines whether or not one is immune to scarlet fever.

 2. Diagnostic tests for some of the diseases have been devised.

  a. The Widal test is an agglutination test used in the diagnosis of typhoid fever.

  b. The Wassermann test, or the Kahn test, is used to determine the presence of syphilis.

  c. For diagnosis of tuberculosis the tuberculin tests in their various forms have been found useful. X-ray pictures are also used to disclose the presence of tuberculosis.

VI. Man is able to exercise some control over his environment to protect himself against the communicable diseases.

 1. The Federal Government has established a Public Health Service which, among other things, studies the problems of communicable disease control.

  a. Provision has been made for campaigns to educate the public in the importance of disease control.

  b. The prevalence, incidence, and mortality rates for communicable and other diseases are compiled.

  c. Research work is sponsored.

  d. Controls for guarding against the importation of diseases from foreign lands have been set up.

 2. The various states have set up their own health departments to help combat diseases.

  a. The New Jersey Health Department has set up certain health regulations intended to help control communicable diseases.

  b. The state department of health passes and enforces regulations concerning the examination of food handlers, standards of purity for milk and other foods, etc.

  c. The state department of health cooperates with the United States Public Health Service in many of its activities.

3. Each community has its own board of health, which acts as a local legislative and executive body for enforcing health regulations.

   a. Millburn Township has a five-man board of health, headed by a local physician.

   b. The Millburn Board of Health functions to prevent the spread of diseases and to control sanitary conditions in the community.

   (1) It passes and enforces quarantine and isolation regulations.

   (2) It passes ordinances regulating conditions under which food may be sold.

   (3) It provides regulation over the keeping of livestock in the township.

   (4) Standards for the purity of the local water supply are drawn up by it.

   (5) It sets up standards for proper plumbing in new buildings and for sewage disposal.

   (6) It provides free immunization service for those who desire it.

   (7) It requires regular cleaning of the township streets.

   (8) It has power to define, investigate, and declare the existence of health hazards in the community.

   (9) It passes ordinances and regulations for standards of sanitation in beauty parlors, barber shops, restaurants, and similar places.

4. Achievement of good health conditions in any community depends upon the cooperation of all its citizens.

   a. When an individual becomes ill, prompt medical attention and early diagnosis of the illness are of value in reducing the severity of some of the communicable diseases.

   b. Prompt recognition of a disease and early medical attention may be of value in controlling an incipient epidemic.

   c. Cooperation with the physician in charge is of value in bringing about quick recovery of the ill person.

   d. The spread of communicable diseases may be minimized by observing quarantine regulations when these are imposed.

   e. Practice of concurrent disinfection is of value in helping to avoid spread of a disease among members of the family.

   f. Practice of terminal disinfection is of value in helping to avoid the spread of communicable disease.

    g. Personal cleanliness and proper hygienic habits are of value in avoiding communicable diseases.

    h. Immunization of all children against diphtheria and smallpox is an effective way of controlling those diseases.

    i. Avoiding crowded places during times of epidemic helps one to escape the dangers of infection.

VII. Science today is investigating unsolved problems of disease control and therapy.

    1. Research is helping man develop methods of control over some of the diseases.

        a. Specific cures are now available for the treatment of some diseases.

           (1) Ehrlich's development of salvarsan for the treatment of syphilis was the first specific chemical drug for a communicable disease to be developed experimentally.

           (2) Before Ehrlich's time quinine had been used as a specific for malaria.

           (3) Sulfonamides are now being used successfully against streptococcic infections, and for such diseases as pneumonia.

        b. Specific drugs are still unavailable for many of our commonest diseases, such as the common cold, influenza, and tuberculosis.

        c. There are many widely advertised and ineffective patented remedies being sold to the public.

ORGANIZATION FOR CLASS PERIODS

After having assembled the learning materials into the unit just outlined, it was deemed advisable to draw up a schedule in which the work was divided into class periods. This schedule was not adhered to rigidly, but it did serve as a study guide for the pupils and prevented the investigator from permitting too much time to be spent on any one phase of the unit. The assignments were mimeographed and given the pupils several days in advance, so that the better learners among them could work at a more rapid pace than the group as a whole.

It will be noticed that throughout this assignment schedule reference is made to "the source unit." This source unit was a mimeographed booklet, prepared by the investigator, enlarging the outline just given. It was written to give the pupils a single source of learning materials in which they could find information they might want. It was made necessary by the fact that no other single source contained all the needed information. As will be seen, however, a number of references were used throughout the learning period.

Assignment Schedule

PERIOD 1

Pretest, Form A

PERIOD 2

Questions and Problems:
1. What are the fundamental problems of human living?
2. How successfully has man solved these problems?
3. How important to man is the problem of good health?
4. How would you define "good health"?
5. In what ways may illness affect the individual? How does it affect the family? What is the effect of illness on the nation?

Activities:
1. Read the following references:* Source Unit, pp. 1–4; Fitzpatrick and Horton, pp. 483–485; Hunter, pp. 455–457; Curtis, Caldwell, and Sherman, pp. 468–469.
2. Make a search of the daily newspapers, of the science magazines in the library and in the laboratory, and other magazines at home, for articles on the importance of the problems of diseases and their control. Read these articles, take notes on them, and report on them in class.

PERIOD 3

Questions and Problems:
1. How may human diseases be classified?
2. What are some examples of each class of diseases?
3. What is meant by communicable diseases?
4. Which communicable diseases are common in the United States? In Millburn? Which are not common?
5. Which of the communicable diseases would you pick for study in this class? Why would you pick these? What would you like to know about them?

---

* The Bibliography at the end of this chapter gives a list of the books and other references cited here. The method of citation used here was found adequate for pupil use.

Activities:

1. Read the USPHS* booklet "Communicable Diseases," pp. 1–3. Read also those parts of the Source Unit, pp. 1–4, which will give you help with the above problems. Also read "Health Through the Ages," pp. 3–29.
2. Find out from the local Board of Health the number and kind of communicable diseases which have been common in Millburn.
3. By using the USPHS reports to be found in the laboratory, find out which diseases have been common in New Jersey during the past five years.
4. By using the USPHS reports, determine the kinds of communicable diseases common in the United States. Which diseases cause most deaths? Of which kinds are there the most cases?
5. Diseases are often reported in terms of the rate per 1,000 population. How do the disease rates for New Jersey compare with the nation as a whole?

PERIOD 4

Questions and Problems:

1. What are the causes of communicable diseases?
2. When were bacteria first seen? By whom?
3. To what group of living things do bacteria belong? Why are they so classified?
4. How large are the largest bacteria? How small are the smallest? Of what importance is this fact?
5. What is the weight of bacteria estimated to be? Why is this important?
6. Where are bacteria found?
7. How are bacteria classified? What are some of the characteristics of each kind?
8. What factors favor the growth of bacteria?
9. In what ways are some kinds of bacteria useful to man?

Activities:

1. Read the following references: Source Unit, pp. 6–8; Fitzpatrick and Horton, pp. 98, 122–124, 25, 483, 460–463; Hunter, 461–463; Smith, pp. 292–298; Curtis, Caldwell, and Sherman, pp. 470–472; Baker, Mills, pp. 96–101; Kinsey, pp. 295–297.
2. Study the lantern slides of bacteria. These are in the laboratory. What did you learn about bacteria from them?

* Refers to the United States Public Health Service.

3. If you wish, come in after school to learn to prepare sterile nutrient agar plates on which bacteria will be grown for class study. At the same time make yourself familiar with the Arnold sterilizer and the bacteriological incubator so you will know how they operate.

PERIOD 5

Questions and Problems:

1. How do bacteria reproduce?
2. How rapidly do bacteria reproduce? How do environmental conditions affect the rate of reproduction? What is the importance of the rate of reproduction in the control of communicable diseases?
3. How do bacteria meet unfavorable conditions in their environment? What are spores? How is spore production different from reproduction? What are the advantages to bacteria of spore production?
4. How may bacteria be killed? What are the most practical ways of killing them? What are some disadvantages of these ways of killing bacteria?
5. What are some of the commonly advertised substances for killing bacteria? Are these substances effective?

Activities:

1. Read the following references: Source Unit, pp. 8–9; Fitzpatrick and Horton, pp. 487–489; Hunter, pp. 458–461; Curtis, Caldwell, and Sherman, pp. 478–481; Moon, Mann, 637–639.
2. Use the prepared nutrient agar plates to show presence of bacteria in the atmosphere, on fingers, on common objects, in drinking water, etc. Expose some plates to a cough. Streak a plate with a throat swab. Keep one plate sterile, as a check. Incubate all these for forty-eight hours; then examine again. What do you find?
3. Inoculate several plates with bacteria. Your teacher will show you how. Immediately expose some of the inoculated plates to direct sunlight with the cover of the plate off; keep others away from sunlight. Then incubate both sets of plates for forty-eight hours. What did you find? How do you explain the results?
4. Bring to class a number of popular disinfectants and antiseptics. Take an equal number of inoculated plates. Soak squares of paper, one-half inch on each side, in the disinfectants and antiseptics, and place them on the inoculated plates. Incubate these for forty-eight hours together with

one plate which has been inoculated but which contains an untreated square of paper. What do you find?

PERIOD 6

Questions and Problems:

1. What are Protozoa? Where are they found?
2. What kinds of Protozoa cause diseases? Which diseases found in this country do they produce?
3. What other human diseases are produced by Protozoa?

Activities:

1. Read the following references: Source Unit, p. 11; Fitzpatrick and Horton, pp. 502–503; Hunter, pp. 482–487; Curtis, Caldwell, and Sherman, pp. 504–506; Smith, pp. 295–301; Baker, Mills, p. 101; Kinsey, p. 318.
2. Make a study of the life cycle of malaria Protozoa life cycles, of the African sleeping sickness Protozoa life cycles. Report what you have learned to your class.

PERIOD 7

Questions and Problems:

1. What are filtrable viruses?
2. How may it be proved that filtrable viruses exist?
3. What diseases are caused by filtrable viruses?
4. What are inclusion bodies? Where are they found?
5. What are the characteristics of the Spirochetes?
6. Which important disease is caused by a Spirochete?
7. What are Rickettsiae? What are their characteristics? Name some diseases caused by them.

Activities:

1. Read the following references: Source Unit, pp. 12–13; Fitzpatrick and Horton, pp. 495–496; Hunter, pp. 479–481; Kinsey, pp. 320–321; Baker, Mills, pp. 101–102; Smith, pp. 224; 298–300.
2. Search through the science magazines in the laboratory or in the library for recent articles on filtrable viruses and Rickettsiae. Report what you have found to your class, or make a brief written report.

PERIOD 8

Questions and Problems:

1. What is the meaning of the term "communicable" in relation to disease?
2. What is meant by "sources of infection"?
3. What are the sources of infection for the common communicable diseases?

4. What can be done to help prevent the spread of infection from its source?

Activities:

1. Read the Source Unit, pp. 13–14.
2. Make a chart of the sources of infection of the common communicable diseases.

PERIOD 9

Questions and Problems:

1. What is meant by "transmission of diseases"?
2. What is meant by transmission of diseases by personal contact? Which disease may be transmitted this way?
3. How may eating utensils convey disease organisms?
4. What disease organisms may be conveyed by water? By milk? Which foods may convey disease organisms? How may this be prevented?
5. Why should we use a handkerchief when coughing or sneezing?
6. How does personal cleanliness help prevent communicable diseases?
7. Why should you have your own personal towel? Washcloth? Drinking glass? Toilet articles?
8. Which insects convey disease organisms? How do they do this? Which diseases do they transmit?
9. What diseases are conveyed to man by mammals? Which diseases may be conveyed to man by other animals?

Activities:

1. Read the following references: Source Unit, p. 12; Hunter, pp. 463–464; Curtis, Caldwell, and Sherman, pp. 472–477; Moon, Mann, pp. 643–645; Kinsey, pp. 324–331, 332–341; Baker, Mills, pp. 108–109, 112–114.
2. Draw some original posters illustrating ways in which diseases are transmitted and suggesting how such transmission may be prevented.
3. Using the prepared slides found in the laboratory, make a microscopic study of the structure of a housefly. Make drawings of those parts of the fly which you think are of importance in the transmission of diseases.

PERIOD 10

Questions and Problems:

1. What is meant by the "period of incubation" of communicable diseases?
2. What are the periods of incubation of the common diseases?

3. What is meant by the "period of communicability" of the diseases?
4. What are the periods of communicability of the common diseases?
5. Of what use is the knowledge about periods of incubation and communicability?

Activities:

1. Read the following reference: Source Unit, pp. 14–15.
2. Make a list of the periods of incubation of the common diseases.
3. Make a list of the periods of communicability of the common diseases.

PERIOD 11

Questions and Problems:

1. What is meant by immunity to a disease?
2. What is "natural" immunity?
3. What is meant by "susceptibility" to a disease?
4. During what seasons of the year are the various diseases most prevalent?
5. Why are some diseases more prevalent at some seasons than at others?
6. Which diseases have a low prevalence in the United States? Why is this so?
7. Which diseases are most prevalent among children? Which are commonest among adults? How do you explain this?
8. Why are some diseases much more common among Negroes than among whites?

Activities:

1. Read the following references: Source Unit, pp. 15–16; also read from "The Control of Communicable Diseases," USPHS Bulletin No. 1697, and "Communicable Diseases," USPHS Miscellaneous Publication No. 30, to find answers to the above problems.
2. Draw up a list of children's communicable diseases; a second list of diseases common to both adults and children; and a third list of diseases more prevalent among adults. Try to find reasons for the variations in the prevalence of these diseases among persons of different ages.

PERIOD 12

Questions and Problems:

1. Taking the common cold, influenza, and pneumonia, be able to answer the following questions about each of them:

a. What are the symptoms of the disease?
b. What causes the disease?
c. What is the source of infection for each?
d. How is each transmitted?
e. What is the period of incubation?
f. What is the period of communicability?
g. Who is susceptible to the disease?
h. When, where, and in what age group is each disease most prevalent?

Activities:
1. Read the following references: Source Unit, pp. 18, 19, 21; "Communicable Diseases," pp. 15–17, 33–35, 49–51; "Colds, Influenza, and Pneumonia," the Metropolitan Life Insurance Company pamphlet; Fitzpatrick and Horton, p. 296; Baker, Mills, pp. 104–105.

PERIOD 13
Questions and Problems:
1. Using the questions given for Period 12, apply them to the diseases diphtheria, measles, and mumps.

Activities:
1. Read the following references: Source Unit, pp. 17, 20, 21; "Communicable Diseases," pp. 19–24, 44–45, 67–69; Metropolitan Life Insurance Company pamphlets on Measles, Diphtheria; Smith, pp. 307–310.

PERIOD 14
Questions and Problems:
1. Using the questions given for Period 12, apply them to the diseases whooping cough, chicken pox, and scarlet fever.

Activities:
1. Read the following references: Source Unit, pp. 17, 21; "Communicable Diseases," pp. 45–46, 70–72, 92–93; Metropolitan Life Insurance Company pamphlets on Scarlet Fever, Whooping Cough.

PERIOD 15
Questions and Problems:
1. Using the questions given for Period 12, apply them to the diseases tuberculosis, gonorrhea, and syphilis.

Activities:
1. Read the following references: Source Unit, pp. 18, 22; 23–24; "Communicable Diseases," pp. 27–31, 73–76, 83–86:

Metropolitan Life Insurance Company pamphlets, Tuberculosis: The Great Imitator; Fitzpatrick and Horton, pp. 492–494; Hunter, pp. 464–466; Curtis, Caldwell, and Sherman, pp. 498–502.

PERIOD 16

Questions and Problems:

1. Using the questions given for Period 12, apply them to the diseases malaria, smallpox, and typhoid fever.

Activities:

1. Read the following references: Source Unit, pp. 19, 22, 24; "Communicable Diseases," pp. 36–39, 87–90, 93–96; Metropolitan Life Insurance Company pamphlets on Malaria, Smallpox, Typhoid Fever; Fitzpatrick and Horton, pp. 479–480, 519–521; Hunter, pp. 466–469, 482–486, 490–492, 495; Curtis, Caldwell, and Sherman, pp. 495–498, 504–506; Smith, pp. 304–306.

PERIOD 17

Questions and Problems:

1. How does the skin protect us against disease organisms?
2. Under what circumstances does the skin fail to protect us against disease organisms?
3. What protection against disease microorganisms is afforded us in the nose, throat, mouth, and windpipe?
4. What is the effect of the hydrochloric acid in the stomach on disease microorganisms?
5. Through what parts of the body do disease organisms most frequently enter? How do they make their entry?

Activities:

1. Read the following references: Source Unit, pp. 25–26; Moon, Mann, pp. 625–627; Baker, Mills, pp. 115–116; "Communicable Diseases" (see each of the diseases).
2. Study the model of the cross-section of the skin in the laboratory. How is the skin adapted to keeping pathogens out of the body?
3. Study the model of the cross-section of the head to determine the passage of air from the nose and mouth to the windpipe. What protection against disease germs is found along this route?

PERIOD 18

Questions and Problems:

1. What happens when pathogens invade the body?

2. How do white corpuscles help the body fight disease germs?
3. What are toxins? What produces them? How does the body overcome them?
4. What are lysins? Agglutinins? Precipitins? Opsonins? What do they do?
5. What do we mean when we say that antibodies are specific?
6. Why are we sometimes immune to a disease after having had it?

Activities:
1. Read the following references: Source Unit, pp. 26–27; Fitzpatrick and Horton, pp. 496–497; Hunter, pp. 386–388, 390–391; Smith, pp. 312–313; Curtis, Caldwell, and Sherman, p. 382; Baker, Mills, pp. 116–118.
2. Study with a microscope the prepared slides of the human blood to be found in the laboratory. Do you find any white corpuscles? If so, make enlarged drawings of them.
3. Using the directions found in Hunter, observe an Amoeba in fission, in movement, and ingesting food, if possible. Compare this with what you know about white corpuscles.
4. Study carefully the films "Man Against Microbe" and "Body Defense Against Disease" when they are shown. What did you like best about these films?

PERIOD 19

Questions and Problems:
1. How can we help the body to become more resistant to diseases?
2. What is meant by "natural" immunity to a disease?
3. What is "acquired" immunity? In what ways may immunity be acquired?
4. What is active acquired immunity? How may it be developed? Which diseases result in active acquired immunity?
5. What is passive acquired immunity? How is it acquired?
6. How is diphtheria antitoxin produced? How is it used?

Activities:
1. Read the following references: Source Unit, pp. 26–28; Fitzpatrick and Horton, pp. 488–490; Hunter, pp. 476–482; Smith, pp. 309–312; Baker, Mills, pp. 118–123; Moon, Mann, pp. 627–634; Curtis, Caldwell, and Sherman, pp. 482–488.
2. Investigate how smallpox vaccine and typhoid vaccine are produced. Report your findings to your class, or make a written report.

3. Make drawings of some of the various types of instruments used in immunizing persons, and explain their use to class.

PERIOD 20

Questions and Problems:

1. For which of the communicable diseases do we have effective means of immunization?
2. For which of the diseases is artificial immunization less effective?
3. For which of the diseases is there no known means of immunization?
4. For which diseases do we have tests of immunity? Of what value are such tests?
5. For which of these diseases do we have diagnostic tests? How are these tests given? What is the value of such tests?
6. What are the laws concerning immunization to communicable diseases in Millburn?

Activities:

1. Read the following references: Source Unit, pp. 29–30; Hunter, pp. 390–391, 478–479; Moon, Mann, pp. 630–631, 634; Baker, Mills, pp. 118–123.
2. In an encyclopedia or reference book, make a special study of the Widal test for typhoid, Schick test for diphtheria, Dick test for scarlet fever, Wassermann test for syphilis, or the tuberculin test for tuberculosis. Try to learn something of the history of these tests, how and when they are used, and the value of each.
3. Find out what the school regulations concerning immunization to smallpox and diphtheria are in Millburn.
4. From the school nurse, find out the results of the patch testing for tuberculosis of the student body. Also have her show you some of the X-ray photographs of pupils' chests, taken last year. What did you learn from this testing program about the prevalence of tuberculosis among your fellow-pupils?

PERIOD 21

Questions and Problems:

1. Why is prompt medical attention important in the treatment of communicable diseases?
2. Why is it important to follow the physician's advice exactly?
3. Why should an ill person remain in bed until he is fully recovered?
4. On what basis should the family physician be selected?

5. Why is it undesirable to try to treat an illness without a physician's advice?
6. Is it desirable to take unprescribed patent drugs and medicines? Give reasons for your answers.
7. Is it desirable to take prescriptions made for another person? Is it desirable to take prescriptions given in some previous illness?

Activities:
1. Read the following references: Source Unit, pp. 31–32; Hunter, pp. 355–358; Baker, Mills, pp. 147–153; Curtis, Caldwell, and Sherman, pp. 512–514, 532–535.
2. Make a search of newspaper, magazine, billboard, and radio advertising of patent medicines. Study the claims made. What do you think of such claims? What are the reasons for your opinions?

PERIOD 22

Questions and Problems:
1. What is meant by "isolation" in the case of a communicable disease? Why is isolation necessary for some diseases?
2. What is meant by "quarantine"? Why is quarantine sometimes necessary?
3. What are the isolation and quarantine regulations in Millburn?
4. How well observed are these regulations?
5. Upon what factor does the length of quarantine depend?
6. Upon what factor does the length of isolation depend?
7. What can be done to avoid contracting a communicable disease during an epidemic?

Activities:
1. Read the following references: Source Unit, pp. 32–33; Hunter, pp. 471–473; Moon, Mann, pp. 639–640; Baker, Mills, p. 125; Curtis, Caldwell, and Sherman, p. 481.
2. Secure a copy of the recently revised township sanitary code. Study it carefully, noting what the periods of quarantine and isolation for the various diseases are.

PERIOD 23

Questions and Problems:
1. What has been the effect of widespread smallpox vaccination on the number of cases of that disease in the United States?
2. Why does smallpox still occur? Should smallpox vaccination be made compulsory everywhere? Why do you think so?

3. What has been the effect of diphtheria immunization on the incidence of that disease? Why does diphtheria still occur? Should immunization against it be made compulsory everywhere? Why?
4. Why are some persons prejudiced against disease immunization? Are their prejudices well based? What are the reasons for your answer?
5. Why is it important to keep records of the number of cases of communicable diseases? Who keeps such records?
6. What use is made of this information?

Activities:

1. Read the following references: Source Unit, p. 33; Fitzpatrick and Horton, pp. 497–498; Hunter, pp. 479–480; Baker, Mills, p. 139; Smith, p. 305.
2. Study the USPHS reports entitled "Prevalence and Incidence of Communicable Diseases" and compare the number of cases of diphtheria, smallpox, or typhoid fever in 1914, 1915, and 1916, with 1937, 1938, and 1939. What do you find? How do you account for your findings?
3. Find out how many in your biology class have been immunized for smallpox or diphtheria. What do you find?

PERIOD 24

Questions and Problems:

1. Why is the home an important consideration in a study of communicable diseases?
2. If there is a case of communicable disease in your home, what can be done to prevent the spread of the disease to other members of the family?
3. What can you do to help prevent the spread of the disease?
4. What is meant by concurrent disinfection?
5. If someone in your home has just recovered from a communicable disease, what can be done to make the home safe for others in it?
6. Why is personal cleanliness important in avoiding disease?

Activities:

1. Read the following references: Source Unit, p. 34; Hunter, pp. 497–500.
2. Make a list of the things that can be done to help prevent the spread of illness from one member of the family to others. Then check this list against what is done in your home, without saying anything about it to other members of your family. How do you rate?

3. Make a list of the things you yourself can do to help avoid diseases, or to avoid passing your own illness to others. Then honestly check yourself to see whether or not you are actually doing these things. How do you rate?

PERIOD 25

Questions and Problems:

1. What is done in Millburn to assure a safe water supply?
2. What provisions are made here for sewage disposal? Why is proper sewage disposal necessary to good health in the community?
3. How does Millburn Township provide for garbage and rubbish disposal?
4. Why does the township have ordinances against keeping livestock in closely inhabited areas?
5. What are the local milk standards? Are these higher or lower than those required by the state? What are the standards for the sale of raw milk?
6. Why are dogs and cats not permitted in local food shops?
7. Why must food handlers be given physical examinations?

Activities:

1. Read the following references: Source Unit, pp. 35–36; Millburn Township Sanitary Code, Revision of 1941; Fitzpatrick and Horton, pp. 498–500; Hunter, pp. 490–492, 503–507; Smith, pp. 314–315; Baker, Mills, pp. 127–129.

PERIOD 26

Questions and Problems:

1. What is the Federal Government doing to prevent diseases being brought into the United States from foreign countries?
2. How does the government try to prevent the pollution of streams and rivers? Why is this important?
3. Why does the government inspect foods?
4. What is the work of the Pure Food and Drug Administration? Is this a necessary task?

Activities:

1. Read the following references: Source Unit, pp. 36–37; also one or more of the monthly Pure Food and Drug Administration reports to be found in the laboratory.

PERIOD 27

Questions and Problems:

1. What are some of the reasons for the widespread incidence of disease in this country?

2. Do all our citizens have the benefit of adequate medical care? Why not?
3. How do many of our cities try to promote good health?
4. What is "socialized medicine"? Do you believe in it?
5. What are the "3-cents-a-day" hospitalization plans? What benefits do they provide?
6. Is sickness and accident insurance desirable? How much does it cost? What are some of the provisions of such insurance?
7. What is the estimated loss to the nation caused by bad health? Why is this of special importance today? Which disease is thought to cause the greatest loss of working time?

Activities:
1. Read the Source Unit, pp. 37–38.
2. Search through newspapers and magazines for articles on the cost of ill health to the nation.
3. Visit local drugstores, restaurants, hamburger stands, bakeries, barber shops, grocery stores, and similar places. Quietly and without comment make note of the measures taken to protect the public health. Note also any unsanitary conditions or practices you may see.

Period 28
Questions and Problems:
1. What are some of the recent developments in the treatment of communicable diseases by means of drugs?
2. What are some of the new "chemical bullets" used in fighting diseases? For which diseases are they effective?
3. What precautions must be taken in the use of the new chemical drugs?
4. Which of the diseases are still unsolved human problems?

Activities:
1. To get recent information on the above assignment, you will need to read the various science magazines in the laboratory and in the library, watch the newspapers and magazines at home for such articles, and use any other sources of information which may occur to you.

Period 29
This period is purposely left "open" in the event that the classes are behind schedule. If they are not, it is to be used either for review, or for work on any problems which the pupils find unclear or unsatisfactorily solved.

PERIOD 30
Post-test, Form B.

ILLUSTRATIVE AND STUDY MATERIALS

A variety of study material was available to the pupils in the experimental group. Multiple copies of several high school textbooks were available. Government publications and pamphlets, and bulletins issued by some of the insurance companies, were also at hand. Newspapers and magazines were used as a source of material for study. Two large bulletin boards were employed to display pictures and articles taken from current periodical literature. Most of this was brought in by the pupils.

A list of the various study materials used in the experiment follows:

Reference Books

Fitzpatrick, F. L. and Horton, R. E. *Biology.* Houghton Mifflin Co., 1937.

Hunter, G. W. *Problems in Biology.* American Book Co., 1939.

Smith, Ella T. *Exploring Biology.* Harcourt, Brace and Co., 1939.

Baker, A. O. and Mills, L. H. *Dynamic Biology.* Rand, McNally and Co., 1933.

Moon, T. S. and Mann, P. B. *Biology.* Henry Holt and Co., 1938.

Curtis, F. D., Caldwell, O. W., and Sherman, Nina H. *Everyday Biology.* Ginn and Co., 1940.

Kinsey, A. C. *New Introduction to Biology.* J. B. Lippincott and Co., 1938.

Broadhurst, Jean and Givens, Leila I. *Microbiology Applied to Nursing.* J. B. Lippincott and Co., 1936.

Meyr, Berl Ben. *Your Germs and Mine.* Doubleday, Doran and Co., 1934.

Parran, Thomas. *Shadow on the Land.* Reynal and Hitchcock, 1937.

Crisp, Katherine B. *Be Healthy.* J. B. Lippincott and Co., 1938.

DeKruif, Paul. *Microbe Hunters.* Harcourt, Brace and Co., 1926.

Gould, G. M. *Pocket Medical Dictionary.* P. Blakiston's Sons and Co., 1934.

Bulletins and Pamphlets

Stimson, A. M. *The Communicable Diseases.* Miscellaneous Publication No. 30, United States Public Health Service. Government Printing Office, Washington, D. C., 1939. 25 cents.

Emerson, Haven and others. *The Control of Communicable Diseases.* Reprint No. 1697, Public Health Reports, Vol. 50, No. 32, August 9, 1935. Government Printing Office, Washington, D. C. 5 cents.

United States Public Health Service. Public Health Reports, Vol. 51, No. 29, July 17, 1936. (This issue contains articles on the relative rank of important causes of sickness and death; malaria control work of the Tennessee Valley Authority and others.) 5 cents.

United States Public Health Service. *The Notifiable Diseases, Prevalence in States.* (These are annual reports; those used were for the years 1914–1939.) Government Printing Office, Washington, D. C. 5 cents.

Department of Health, State of New Jersey. *Food and Drug Laws, Revision of 1937.* Circular 211. Department of Health, Trenton, N. J.

Department of Health, State of New Jersey. *Revised Statutes Relating to Waters, Water Supplies, and Sewerage Systems.* Circular 213. Department of Health, Trenton, N. J., 1938.

Department of Health, State of New Jersey. Revised Statutes of New Jersey, Title 26, Circular 210. *Health and Vital Statistics, Together with Extracts from Certain Other Statutes Relating to Public Health.* Department of Health, Trenton, N. J., 1937.

Sanitary Code for Millburn Township, Revision of 1941. Board of Health, Millburn, N. J.

Pamphlets

Metropolitan Life Insurance Company, New York, N. Y. Twenty copies of each of the following were in the laboratory:

Health, Happiness, and Long Life

Health Through the Ages

Just a Cold?—Or—

Diphtheria

Measles

The Conquest of Typhoid Fever

Vaccination Protects You Against Smallpox

Scarlet Fever

Whooping Cough

Tuberculosis

The Great Imitator

Malaria

Cold, Influenza, Pneumonia

Health Hero Series:

Edward Jenner

Robert Koch

Edward L. Trudeau

Louis Pasteur

Walter Reed

Florence Nightingale

Also:
John Hancock Mutual Life Insurance Company, Boston, Massachusetts. *Home Care of Communicable Diseases.* (35 copies)

Newspapers and Magazines

The *New York Herald-Tribune* and the *New York Times* were available in the laboratory, in the pupils' home rooms, and in the library.

Science magazines available in the laboratory and the library were: *Science News Letter, Science Digest, Scientific American,* and *Popular Science.*

Audio-Visual Materials

Motion Pictures:
The House Fly. Eastman Kodak Company, Rochester, N. Y.
Man Against Microbe. Metropolitan Life Insurance Company, N. Y.
Body Defense Against Disease. Erpi Classroom Films, Inc., 35–11 Thirty-fifth Avenue, Long Island City, N. Y.
Understanding Tuberculosis. Erpi Classroom Films, Inc., 35–11 Thirty-fifth Avenue, Long Island City, N. Y.
Understanding Pneumonia. Erpi Classroom Films, Inc., 35–11 Thirty-fifth Avenue, Long Island City, N. Y.

Film Strips:
The Life of Pasteur. Metropolitan Life Insurance Company, New York, N. Y.
The Life of Koch. Metropolitan Life Insurance Company, New York, N. Y.
The Life of Jenner. Metropolitan Life Insurance Company, New York, N. Y.

Lantern Slides:
Photomicrographs of the pathogenic organisms causing the following diseases were used: diphtheria, gonorrhea, malaria, tuberculosis, syphilis, tetanus, typhoid fever, whooping cough, and scarlet fever.

Microscope Slides:
Microscope slides of the bacteria found on the nutrient agar plates prepared in class were made and used. Other microscope slides of the human blood were also used. The microprojector was used to study the movements of the Amoebae in order to compare them with white corpuscles.

Laboratory Equipment

Laboratory equipment used in the experimental teaching of this unit included the following items:

Arnold sterilizer
Bacteriological incubator
5 dozen Pyrex Petri dishes
Platinum wire
1 lb. cotton (for cotton plugs)
¼ lb. Difco Nutrient Agar

Gas burner (on legs, for heating Arnold sterilizer)
5 microscopes, with depression slides, cover glasses, etc.
Quantity of distilled water (for making up the nutritive medium)

Chapter IV

THE INFORMATION TESTS

As has been previously stated, only one paper and pencil test, having two forms, was used in the investigation. These forms were labeled A and B. Form A was used as a pretest; Form B was used at the close of study of the unit on communicable diseases. Then, twelve weeks later, Form A was again given, this time as a retention test. In each instance the control group also took the test.

CONSTRUCTION OF THE TEST

It may be well to give an account of the procedures used in constructing the test. Every effort was made to have items parallel the emphasis given to the various parts of the learning materials. The following steps were followed:

1. A complete list of facts in the "Source Unit" was compiled, each being phrased as a simple declarative sentence.

2. The declarative sentences were then changed into test items. Some of these were of the true-false type, some were multiple-choice items, and others were found most usable as matching questions. A total of 460 items was thus obtained.

3. The 460 items were divided into the two Forms, A and B. The true-false items were divided by drawing from a hat slips of paper on which they were written, alternating statements being assigned to the two forms. The multiple-choice and matching items were for the most part specific questions dealing with the fifteen common communicable diseases which formed the basis for the "Source Unit." These diseases were listed alphabetically. Then seven of them in any particular set

of items were assigned to Form A, every other one being taken. The alternate eight were then assigned to Form B.

4. Each of the two forms of the test was then submitted to a group of seven persons who have some competence in the area of communicable diseases, or education, or both. Two of these were practicing physicians, two were high school biology teachers, one was a New York City Board of Health official with a degree in medicine, one was a member of the Department of Teaching of Natural Sciences in Teachers College, Columbia University, and one was a professor of Bacteriology in the same institution.

Each of these persons read the items, noted which seemed ambiguous, unimportant, or lacking in objectivity, and made out a key for the tests. Agreement of the value of the item and its answer by five of the seven judges* was deemed sufficient to justify including it in the test. A few of the items which failed to meet this requirement were rewritten in the light of the criticisms made, because they seemed too important to discard.

In this way the test was made valid and at the same time a key made out by experts was obtained.

5. These preliminary forms of the test were then given to 100 unselected tenth-year pupils, who during the previous academic year had studied much of the material on which they were based. Their scores were ranked, and the upper and lower quartiles determined. Then practically all the items which failed to distinguish between them were eliminated. The remaining items were then arranged in the order of their difficulty, on a scale ranging from 0 to 1.0, the former figure representing items missed by no pupils, the latter, items missed by all. Items were then selected so that the percentage from each order of difficulty in the test would approximate a normal curve. This left each form with 150 items, which was found to be a suitable length for use in the available class period. It was found that

---

* It was found that in a few instances some of the items were in the area of opinion, the authorities consulted here having so stated.

superior pupils completed the test (either form) in thirty minutes.

6. Upon completion of the revision of the two forms, the same pupils took each of them twice. Form A was given in the morning and afternoon of one day; a week later Form B was given. The papers were scored, and the coefficient of reliability was calculated. The following results were obtained:

Correlation of Form A with itself .... .91
Correlation of Form B with itself .... .90
Correlation of Form A with Form B .... .89

It must be remembered that the above correlations were obtained in the preliminary work, and not with the pupils involved in the experiment here reported. But the control group in the investigation gave an opportunity to check the reliability of the test again. During the course of the investigation these pupils first took Form A; six weeks later they were given Form B. After another twelve weeks had elapsed they again took Form A. The following coefficients of reliability were obtained from these applications of the test:

Correlation of Form A with Form B .... .92
Correlation of Form A with itself .... .97
Correlation of Form B with Form A .... .92

Garrett states that "there is fairly good agreement among workers with psychological and educational tests that an r of . . . .70 to 1.0 denotes high to very high relation."[1] The two forms of the test were therefore deemed sufficiently similar for the use to which they were to be put.

The tests were to be used only to show that learning had taken place, such learning as is measured by such a test. If changes in behavior had not been found, it might have been argued that no kind of learning had taken place.

There is a possibility that the magnitude of the correlations may have been increased by the fact that the two forms of the test contained questions of a parallel nature. For example,

[1] Garrett, H. E., *Statistics in Psychology and Education*, p. 342. Longmans, Green and Co., 1937.

there are questions on the communicability of the diseases, their specific causes, their modes of transmission, and their periods of incubation. It will be recalled that fifteen diseases were studied. A question on eight of these was put in Form A; the same question on the other seven was placed in Form B. This comment applies only to the correlations between the two forms of the test; it may be claimed that the correlations were intrinsically high as was shown when each of the forms was given twice on the same day to the same group, in determining the self-correlations.

The complete tests are given in the Appendix.

Chapter V

OBSERVATION TECHNIQUES AND THE INTERVIEWS

Since the behavior data in this investigation were in large part secured by observations of the pupils in the classroom, and by interviews with them, it is necessary to describe the techniques and procedures used. It will be recalled that the observations were used to determine the extent and character of undesirable behaviors. The interviews were of two kinds, those with all pupils, hereafter called Interview A, and those with pupils who had been absent from school because of communicable illness, which will be referred to as Interview B. Interview A was used to explore certain behaviors in situations outside the classroom, situations which could not be observed directly.

THE OBSERVATIONS

The observations were made in biology and English classes on both the control and the experimental groups. Observations in the English classes were intended to show whether or not the results obtained in biology classes were typical of pupils in other situations, and also to determine whether or not any changes which might occur as a result of learning by the experimental group carried over or took place only in the biology classes.

Reliability of the observations was established by having two observers recording behaviors simultaneously in the biology classes. While pupils carried on their regular work under a student chairman, the two observers (one of whom was the investigator, the other an independent person not associated with the school) took notes on what they saw.

A simple technique was used in recording the observations.

49

The behaviors under consideration (listed in Chapter II) were given numbers, from 1 to 7. Thus, if a pupil was seen to put his finger in his mouth, the observer had but to write the figure 1 on the seating chart he had in hand, in the proper space. This recording did not interfere with the actual observation. The use of a seating chart eliminated the necessity of having second observer learn the pupils' names.

After two weeks of such observations two sets of records for each of the 126 pupils in the study were available. Each pupil's "behavior score" was then arrived at by counting up the undesirable actions he had committed. When the coefficient of correlation between the investigator's observation scores and those of the second observer was calculated, it was found to be .99, indicating a high degree of reliability. Validity of the items of observation was established, as has been explained, by previously submitting the lists for judgment by the group of competent persons mentioned in Chapter II.

Further details of the observation technique may be of value. Each observation period was twenty minutes; there were ten of them. Three of the observations were conducted during the first part of the period, four during the middle of the period, and three at the end of the period. This was done to obtain a cross-section of pupil behavior during the entire class period. Pupils who were absent were observed as soon as they returned to class for a period of time equal to that during which observation on them had been missed.

An attempt was made to keep pupil activity as nearly normal as possible while the observations were going on. On two days the pupils were engaged in study activity and research work on previously made assignments. On two other occasions they were doing written work. During four of the periods oral recitation and discussion occupied their attention, while the other two periods were given to pupil reports.

One series of observations was carried out before the learning materials prepared for this unit were studied by the experimental group; the second came immediately after the close of the unit; the third came twelve weeks later.

Observations in English classes were done by the same observer who had helped establish the reliability coefficient of the observations in biology classes. As in the case of the information test, the control group scores were useful in determining the reliability coefficients of the observations:

r

Coefficient of correlation between first and second observations in biology classes .... .89
Coefficient of correlation between first and third observations in biology classes .... .86
Coefficient of correlation between second and third observations in biology classes .... .94
Coefficient of correlation between first and second observations in English classes .... .88
Coefficient of correlation between first and third observations in English classes .... .94
Coefficient of correlation between second and third observations in English classes .... .94

These high coefficients of correlation indicate not only that the observations were reliable, but that there was a degree of stability in this phase of pupil behavior. Those who did many undesirable things continued to do them; others, relatively free of such behavior, continued to have low scores.

In the English classes work continued under normal circumstances, with the regular teacher cooperating by conducting classes as usual. The observations all took place concurrently.

Pupils were at all times unaware of what was being done. Their curiosity was aroused, of course, when they saw the same observer in both biology and English classes every day for more than two weeks; eventually they arrived at the conclusion that their study habits and recitations were being recorded. When they questioned their English teachers or the investigator about this they were given noncommittal replies.

INTERVIEWS WITH ALL PUPILS

As has been previously stated, there were a number of aspects of behavior which the investigator deemed pertinent to this study but which could not be observed directly. The nature and extent of such behavior was therefore determined by interviews with all pupils, called Interview A.

Interview A was based on the following questions of behavior:

1. Does the pupil wash his hands before eating lunch at school, or during the school week?
2. Does the pupil wash his hands before eating dinner?
3. Does the pupil wash his hands after having been to the toilet at school?
4. Does the pupil wash his hands after having been to the toilet at home?
5. Does the pupil have a towel reserved for his use, and used exclusively by him, at home? Does he use only his own towel?
6. Does the pupil have a washcloth reserved for his use, and used exclusively by him, at home? Does he use only his own washcloth?
7. Does the pupil have a drinking glass for his own personal use, and used only by him, at home? Does he use only his own drinking glass?
8. Does the pupil "take a bite" of food being eaten by another person?
9. Does the pupil "give a bite" to another person of food he is eating?
10. Does the pupil have a clean handkerchief daily?

Each pupil was to be assigned an arbitrary score of 100 points if his behavior was perfect. None such was found. Each question was assigned a value of ten points, but it is obvious that they are not of the kind that can be answered by a flat "yes" or "no." Questions 1, 2, 3, 4, 8, and 9 were therefore scored on the basis of the possibility of one of four answers. If the interview disclosed that a pupil could answer "always" to one of these, he was given full credit of ten points. Other possible answers were "usually" with seven points credit, "sometimes" with four points credit, or "never" with no credit.

Questions 5, 6, and 7 were broken down into two parts. If the interview revealed that, in answer to the conversation about question 5, the pupil had a towel reserved for his own use at home, he was credited with five points. If he always used only his own towel, he was given another five points; but if he said that he "usually" used his own towel he was given three and one-half points; if "sometimes," two points, and if "never" then no points credit were given. The latter points were, of course, in addition to the original five.

Question 10 also was scored on the basis of four possible answers: "daily," with full credit; "almost every day," with seven points; "occasionally" with four points; and "never" with no points credit.

These interviews, like the test and observations, were held in the pre-study, post-study, and retention periods. They were all done by the investigator. In the pre-study period each pupil was interviewed twice within the space of two weeks. Some of the interviews were held during the investigator's "free period"; others, during the "activity period" with those pupils who were not in activities; and the remainder after school hours.

The reliability of the data secured by means of these interviews is indicated by the coefficient of correlation obtained before the two sets of pre-study interview scores. This reliability coefficient was found to be .89. The coefficients were lower when they were calculated for the control group on the basis of data obtained during the course of the experiment. They were as follows:

Coefficient of correlation between first and second Interview A .... .53
Coefficient of correlation between first and third Interview A .... .78
Coefficient of correlation between second and third Interview A .... .54

These correlations, while not so high as those reported for the test and observations, are still sufficiently high to be considered substantial. Part of their lower value may be due to the fact that in the interviews no rigid form was followed; they were informal, friendly, and perhaps too hurried to achieve more perfect results. The two sets of interviews in the pre-study period, those in the post-study period, and those held twelve weeks after the close of the experimental learning totaled 504.

Then, too, it is possible that conversations about these matters may have brought about changes of behaviors in the pupils in the control group on whose scores the last three coefficients were based. There was no way, either, of checking how much influence pupils in the experimental group may have had on the others; there may have been sufficient conversation about the interviews to have affected the results obtained.

It is, of course, also possible that the behavior involved in this part of the study is not so stable as the observed behavior, and that a lower coefficient of reliability is therefore to be expected. Some evidence to this effect may be derived from the much higher correlation between the first two pre-study interviews, in which the time factor was not so pronounced. This coefficient, it will be remembered, was .89.

INTERVIEWS WITH PUPILS ABSENT BECAUSE OF COMMUNICABLE ILLNESS

The final phase of this study involved a scrutiny of the behavior of pupils during communicable illness. As was shown in Chapter II, there was evidence that this part of the investigation should deal with the following questions, on which these interviews were based:

1. Did the pupil remain home from school at the first sign of illness?
2. When the pupil stayed home, did he either return to bed upon arising and feeling ill, or go to bed as soon as he felt ill?
3. Did the pupil remain in bed until fully recovered?
4. When the pupil remained home, was his pulse rate taken?
5. Was the sick pupil's temperature taken?
6. Was a physician called to treat the illness?
7. Did the ill pupil have visitors other than members of his immediate family, when he was ill?
8. Did the pupil take home-prescribed patent medicines?
9. When the pupil was ill, were his eating utensils sterilized, or otherwise properly cared for?
10. Were the pupil's handkerchiefs, if he used them, sterilized?

The pupil's answers to these questions were also scored on the basis of 100 points. The answers here were assumed to be either "yes" or "no." For purposes of this study it was assumed that the pupil, being an adolescent, would be subject to the wishes of his parents in many ways. Therefore, if he indicated that his wishes were contrary to those of his parents, he was credited with what he had wanted. For example, one boy told the interviewer that he had wanted to have a physician, but that his parents did not think he was seriously ill, and therefore did not call a physician despite the fact that the boy wanted one. He was given full credit in his interview score. Nor was it to be expected that ill pupils would rise from their sickbeds to supervise the washing of the dishes which they had used, but if they took notice of whether or not this had been done properly, or testified that they had expressed concern about it, they were given full credit.

These interviews were begun with pupils absent on October 1; all persons absent between that day and January 1 were considered to be in the pre-study period. There were fifty-five such absentees, twenty-six in the experimental group and twenty-nine in the control group. Each of them was interviewed twice in the pre-study period, once immediately upon returning to school and again two days later. The scores made by these pupils were then ranked, and the coefficient of reliability calculated. This was found to be .99, showing that the pupil testimony must have been dependable.

During the six weeks following the opening of school in January, when the experimental group was studying Communicable Diseases, no ill absentees were interviewed. Then, from the middle of February until twelve weeks later, ill pupils were again given Interview B.

Seventeen pupils in the control group who had been absent in the pre-study period were again absent in the latter period. Since they had not studied the unit, they provided some basis for the calculation of a coefficient of correlation between their two sets of scores. This was found to be .47, but it cannot be taken as a true measure of the reliability of the interview because of the small number of cases, the length of time which had elapsed between their first and second illnesses, etc.

There is little doubt in the investigator's mind that the evidence given by these pupils was true; what is likely is that their illnesses varied in severity, that weather conditions may have affected their decision to attend school or not to attend school, and so on. These factors must be borne in mind when attention is given the data presented in Chapter VI. At any rate, an *r* of .47 is not significantly different from zero, since the number of cases was only seventeen. According to Lindquist,[1] the coefficient should be at least .482 to be considered significant at the 5 per cent level, and .606 at the 1 per cent level, with seventeen cases.

It was assumed, therefore, that the data presented in Interview B were reliable at the time they were obtained, but that a pupil's behavior when he was ill one time had no really significant correlation with what he might score later.

Validity of the material included in Interview B was achieved by submitting the points on which the interviews were based and on which pupils were scored to the seven competent persons mentioned previously in Chapter II.

While other data in this investigation are presented in pre-study, post-study, and retention periods, this was not possible with Interview B because pupils were not absent in sufficiently large numbers. Therefore the data are presented simply as pre-study and post-study information. In the post-study period thirty pupils were absent because of communicable illness from the experimental group, and a like number from the control group.

It may be recognized at this point that perhaps the validity of the data secured by means of the interviews may be debatable. The procedure of using an external criterion as a means of judging validity could have been applied to this phase of the study only with extreme difficulty. Nevertheless, the results obtained with the experimental group are at least a strong indication that the interviews show the trend and direction of the changes which took place.

[1] Lindquist, E. F., *Statistical Analysis in Educational Research*, pp. 210–213. Houghton Mifflin Co., Boston, 1940.

Chapter VI

DATA OF THE EXPERIMENT

COMPARABILITY OF EXPERIMENTAL AND CONTROL GROUPS

SINCE two groups of pupils were involved in this experiment, one functioning as a control and the other being experimental, it is necessary to establish the comparability of the pupils at the beginning of the study. Table II shows how the two groups compared in grade level, sex distribution, age, and intelligence. Table III summarizes the comparability of the two groups in the experimental factors, giving data on the information tests, observations of behavior in both biology and English classes, and the two interviews. It will be noted that the control group was slightly older than the experimental and that it made a somewhat better mean on the information pretest and somewhat better scores in the observed behaviors as well as in the interviews.

TABLE II

GRADE LEVEL, SEX DISTRIBUTION, AGE, AND INTELLIGENCE QUOTIENTS OF EXPERIMENTAL AND CONTROL GROUPS

Group		Grade		Sex		Age[1]		I.Q.[2]	
	N	9th	10th	Boys	Girls	M	SD	M	SD
Experimental	62	58	4	33	29	14–3.0	7.36	108.09	9.66
Control	64	57	7	36	28	14–5.5	8.52	108.80	10.50

[1] Age is given in years and months as of October 1, 1941.
[2] I.Q. was obtained with Otis Self-Administering Test.

GAINS IN EXPERIMENTAL FACTORS

The gains in information and the changes in the behaviors occurring during the course of the study are shown in Table IV.

TABLE III

Comparability of the Control and Experimental Groups

In Scores on Information Test, Observations, and Behavior as Determined by Interviews

Group	Pretest		Observations[1]				Interview A		Interview B	
			Biology		English					
	M	SD	M	SD	M	SD	M	SD	M	SD
Experimental	78.58	11.21	18.26	13.35	23.48	17.59	64.34	15.43	41.92	16.67
Control	82.09	10.47	17.02	11.47	23.11	13.36	67.26	12.28	46.90	16.53
Differences in means..	-3.51		1.24		0.37		-2.92		-4.98	

[1] "Biology" and "English" refer to classes in which observations were made.

TABLE IV

Changes in Scores of Experimental and Control Groups, Showing Data Obtained in Pre-study, Post-study, and Retention Periods

Group and Period	Information Test		Observed Behaviors				Interview A		Interview B	
			Biology		English					
	M	SD	M	SD	M	SD	M	SD	M	SD
Experimental										
Pre-study	78.58	11.21	18.26	13.35	23.48	17.59	64.34	15.43	41.92	16.67
Post-study	122.03	11.39	3.48	2.88	7.55	6.49	74.60	19.95	...	...
Retention	103.18	10.69	3.65	2.28	7.95	5.50	74.00	14.98	61.33	20.13
Gain*	24.60		14.61		15.53		9.66		20.41	
Control										
Pre-study	82.09	10.47	17.02	11.47	23.11	13.36	67.26	12.28	46.90	16.53
Post-study	87.03	11.38	19.48	12.30	23.39	14.08	65.70	17.10	...	...
Retention	84.73	11.01	20.16	11.65	23.02	11.60	68.58	13.33	45.00	20.66
Gain*	2.64		-3.14		0.09		1.42		-1.90	

* Differences in means between pre-study and retention periods of taking observations and interviews.

The control group shows a gain of 4.94 on the information test in the post-study period. Some of this gain may be attributed to the fact that during the study every pupil was patch-tested for tuberculosis. Before this was done every pupil in the school who was to be tested attended a forty-five-minute lecture on the disease and saw a motion picture on it. Following this came a period of questioning, during which the control as well as experimental pupils had opportunity to discuss the problems of tuberculosis control. Their interest was brought to the various biology classes, and some learning consequently may have occurred.

Another factor which could not be eliminated from the study was the exchange of experiences carried on between pupils of the two groups. It must be remembered that they were segregated only in their biology classes, and that in many cases they were neighbors and well acquainted with each other. As a result of this, pupils in the experimental group undoubtedly shared their experiences with those in the control group, so that the latter learned from the former. This factor may have influenced other aspects of the study as well.

It will also be seen from Table IV that the experimental group shows a considerable rise in the mean score on the information test in the post-study period, when it was given immediately after close of study of the unit. Much of this gain was lost when the test was given again in the retention period twelve weeks later. It is significant to observe, however, that the gains of the experimental pupils in the observed behavior and in the items included in Interview A were maintained with but very little loss. This would seem to indicate that while some of the information on which the changes were based was lost, the changes in behavior tended to show a high degree of permanency. Perhaps the lower scores on the information test were at least partly due to boredom resulting from repetition, and partly due to the fact that pupils understood that the test would have no bearing on their grades in the course.

Table IV also shows that in the behavior scores determined by Interview B (pupils absent from school because of communicable illness) the experimental group showed a gain which could not be matched by the control pupils. In this connection it must be mentioned again that of the twenty-six experimental pupils who were absent because of illness in the pre-study period, seventeen were absent for the same reason in the post-study period. Here, then, was a group which made available data useful in comparing behavior at the two different times. The pre-study mean score of this segment was 41.18 as compared with 41.92 for the twenty-six absentees as a whole. Their post-study score was 61.33 as compared with the mean score of 62.35 made by thirty pupils in their group absent because of illness.

A similar number of pupils was absent because of communicable illness in both the pre-study and the post-study periods in the control classes. The pre-study mean score for the seventeen was 42.94 as compared with 46.90 for all; their post-study mean score was 44.12 against 45.00 for all absentees in their classes.

Thus we have an experimental group of seventeen pupils and a control group of seventeen pupils, both absent in the pre-study and post-study periods. The control group mean score showed a gain of 1.18; the difference between the two means of the experimental segment was 20.15.

ANALYSIS OF CHANGES IN BEHAVIOR OBSERVED IN BIOLOGY AND ENGLISH CLASSES

Tables V and VI show the frequency of occurrence of the various observed behaviors in both groups in the pre-study, post-study, and retention periods; one table gives the results of observations in biology classes and the other in English classes. It must be remembered that the observer of English classes had been trained before any observations had been made, and had previously helped establish the reliability of the observations in biology classes, which turned out to be .99. There can be little doubt, therefore, that the scores obtained in English classes were highly reliable; that they were also considerably higher is interesting, but the point was not further investigated. The gains made by the experimental group may be described as very great, as comparison with their own previous scores and with those of the control group shows.

TABLE V

CHANGES IN FIVE BEHAVIORS AS OBSERVED IN BIOLOGY CLASSES

Behavior	No. of Cases					
	Pre-study		Post-study		Retention	
	Exp.	Cont.	Exp.	Cont.	Exp.	Cont.
Fingers in mouth	692	717	163	739	172	813
Other objects in mouth ..	237	217	16	272	16	229
Fingernail biting	44	61	4	90	6	73
Fingers in nostrils	60	27	8	51	2	48
Rubbing eye with finger ..	99	67	25	96	30	129
Total	1132	1089	216	1248	226	1292

TABLE VI

CHANGES IN FIVE BEHAVIORS AS OBSERVED IN ENGLISH CLASSES

Behavior	No. of Cases					
	Pre-study		Post-study		Retention	
	Exp.	Cont.	Exp.	Cont.	Exp.	Cont.
Fingers in mouth	907	941	283	888	327	860
Other objects in mouth ...	290	241	111	304	107	317
Fingernail biting	63	43	7	61	6	57
Finger in nostril	41	58	7	63	5	55
Rubbing eye with finger ..	155	196	60	181	48	184
Total	1456	1479	468	1497	493	1473

Study of Tables V and VI shows that not only did the experimental group change in its behavior, but these changes were evident in classes other than those involved in the experiment, and the changes were more than temporary.

Because so many of the diseases studied were respiratory infections, observations on the use of handkerchiefs when coughing and sneezing were of special significance. Tables VII and VIII give data on the use of the handkerchief when coughing in the biology and English classes respectively; Tables IX and X give data on the use of handkerchiefs when sneezing in the same situations. The two behaviors are treated separately because experimental pupils in their consideration of the importance of using a handkerchief were prone to contend that sneezes came too quickly for proper use of the precautions they recognized as having value. Other pupils answered this point by maintaining that there really was time for getting the handkerchief once the habit of doing so was established. Therefore, for purposes of this study, the two behaviors are shown separately.

TABLE VII

USE OF HANDKERCHIEF WHEN COUGHING IN BIOLOGY CLASSES, EXPERIMENTAL AND CONTROL GROUPS

Group	No. of Pupils Coughing	No. of Coughs	Handkerchief Not Used	Handkerchief Used	% Use of Handkerchief
Experimental					
Pre-study	32	221	221	0	0%
Post-study	22	101	18	83	82
Retention	27	81	17	64	79
Control					
Pre-study	29	116	116	0	0
Post-study	29	129	129	0	0
Retention	26	67	65	2	3

TABLE VIII

USE OF HANDKERCHIEF WHEN COUGHING IN ENGLISH CLASSES, EXPERIMENTAL AND CONTROL GROUPS

Group	No. of Pupils Coughing	No. of Coughs	Handkerchief Not Used	Handkerchief Used	% Use of Handkerchief
Experimental					
Pre-study	27	234	234	0	0%
Post-study	24	94	21	73	78
Retention	23	46	11	35	76
Control					
Pre-study	20	66	66	0	0
Post-study	23	89	88	1	1.1
Retention	20	55	55	0	0

TABLE IX

Use of Handkerchief When Sneezing in Biology Classes,
Experimental and Control Groups

Group	No. of Pupils Sneezing	No. of Sneezes	Handker-chief Not Used	Handker-chief Used	% Use of Handker-chief
Experimental					
Pre-study	12	27	23	4	14.8%
Post-study	12	19	3	16	84.2
Retention	11	21	3	18	85.7
Control					
Pre-study	12	14	13	1	7.1
Post-study	11	17	15	2	11.8
Retention	10	12	11	1	8.3

TABLE X

Use of Handkerchief When Sneezing in English Classes,
Experimental and Control Groups

Group	No. of Pupils Sneezing	No. of Sneezes	Handker-chief Not Used	Handker-chief Used	% Use of Handker-chief
Experimental					
Pre-study	10	14	14	0	0%
Post-study	12	19	10	9	48.4
Retention	13	17	7	10	58.8
Control					
Pre-study	11	16	16	0	0
Post-study	9	11	10	1	9.1
Retention	9	13	13	0	0

In summarizing the data presented thus far it may be said that it has been shown that the two groups were similar enough for purposes of comparison in this experiment not only in their general characteristics but in the behavior studied also; that the experimental group made gains which the control group could not match, and that while the experimental group did not retain all its initial margin shown in the information post-test, it did retain the changes it had made in the observed behaviors and in those determined by Interview B, as well as much of its gain in Interview A.

ANALYSIS OF CHANGES IN BEHAVIOR AS
DETERMINED BY INTERVIEW A

Tables XI to XX, inclusive, give information on the various changes as determined by what has been called Interview A. It will be seen that the changes in this phase of the study are not so pronounced as in the observed behavior. For example, it was found that the experimental group made some gains in all the behaviors, but not so much as might have been expected. This may have been due to a number of reasons. Pupils said that they did not wash their hands before lunch because if they did so they would be late coming into the cafeteria and so would not have as wide a choice of food as they would have if they rushed for their lunch immediately upon dismissal from classes. According to the testimony of many of them, a lunch period of thirty-three minutes was not long enough for both eating and washing their hands. This was not really true, for the cafeteria was found to be deserted ten minutes before afternoon classes began. While the pupils' classroom experiences with culture plates inoculated with bacteria from their fingers were apparently convincing enough to deter many from putting their fingers into their mouths, they were not sufficient to prevent them from eating with unwashed hands. In the conflict between hunger and hygiene, hunger proved to be the stronger factor. Some of this rush to get to the cafeteria was probably due to the fact that, with school beginning at 8:20 in the morning, many pupils did not take the time to eat a proper breakfast. No doubt by noon they were truly famished. Even so, the number of experimental pupils who never washed their hands before lunch dropped from thirty-one in the pre-study period to eleven in the post-study period. However, a surprising number of control pupils also made this change; several of them ascribed their more frequent practice of this behaviorism to conversations about "germs" with experimental pupils. Others testified that "Mother has been after me lately to wash my hands before I eat."

Table XI shows that practically all people in both groups wash their hands before dinner, but the experimental group showed a gain of thirteen pupils who wash their hands regularly before their evening meal, while the control group showed a decline of four. Tables XII, XIII, and XIV give similar results.

It was interesting to discover that of the sixty-two pupils in the experimental group, twenty-five came from homes in which individual members of the family were not assigned personal towels. All of these pupils said that in their homes it was customary to place one or more towels on a rack in the bathroom, and that these were used indiscriminately. Eight of these pupils were sufficiently motivated by their study of communicable diseases to have towels reserved for themselves. But the number who had a personal washcloth showed no similar change. There was, however, an increase in the frequency of use of their own washcloths in the experimental group and none in the control group.

Experimental pupils also were less inclined to share food which was being eaten; that is, they were less likely to "take a bite," or to "give a bite," as they expressed it. Here again it was found that external circumstances tended to limit the changes which might have occurred. Social considerations were found to be a strong influence. One pupil said: "When you're eating a bar of candy, and a kid comes along and asks you for some, you can't say no. He'll think you're stingy or something." Another pupil in the experimental group said, "Sure, we know that giving somebody a bite of what you're eating isn't right, but the other guy who hasn't studied diseases doesn't know that. He thinks you just don't want to give him any, and you can't explain. He doesn't think about germs."

In other behaviors the home environment was found to act as a check on changes which otherwise might have occurred. One girl said in an interview that it would be nice if all members of her family had a towel assigned to them, but that her mother was not strong enough to do the big washing which would result. Another said that her family did not have sufficient towels to follow this practice. A boy testified in an interview that his father thought that "what children learn in school nowadays is mostly nonsense; on the farm when I was a boy we all drank out of the same bucket and used the same dipper, and I'm still here."

Thus there is evidence that the changes listed in the tables giving data on behavior as determined by Interview A are limited by factors over which the child does not have a large

TABLE XI

WASHING HANDS BEFORE LUNCH, EXPERIMENTAL AND CONTROL GROUPS

Time of Interview	Experimental Group				Control Group			
	Always Wash	Usually Wash	Seldom Wash	Never Wash	Always Wash	Usually Wash	Seldom Wash	Never Wash
Pre-study	2	7	22	31	1	2	31	30
Post-study	3	19	35	5	1	12	32	19
Retention	5	20	26	11	2	9	34	19

TABLE XII

WASHING HANDS BEFORE DINNER, EXPERIMENTAL AND CONTROL GROUPS

Time of Interview	Experimental Group				Control Group			
	Always Wash	Usually Wash	Seldom Wash	Never Wash	Always Wash	Usually Wash	Seldom Wash	Never Wash
Pre-study	35	25	2	0	33	27	4	0
Post-study	41	19	2	0	26	31	7	0
Retention	48	12	2	0	29	30	5	0

TABLE XIII

WASHING HANDS AFTER HAVING BEEN TO TOILET AT HOME,
EXPERIMENTAL AND CONTROL GROUPS

Time of Interview	Experimental Group				Control Group			
	Always Wash	Usually Wash	Seldom Wash	Never Wash	Always Wash	Usually Wash	Seldom Wash	Never Wash
Pre-study	32	21	8	1	31	25	8	0
Post-study	42	17	2	1	34	20	9	1
Retention	43	15	4	0	31	21	11	1

TABLE XIV

WASHING HANDS AFTER HAVING BEEN TO TOILET AWAY FROM HOME,
EXPERIMENTAL AND CONTROL GROUPS

Time of Interview	Experimental Group				Control Group			
	Always Wash	Usually Wash	Seldom Wash	Never Wash	Always Wash	Usually Wash	Seldom Wash	Never Wash
Pre-study	25	19	14	4	27	24	11	2
Post-study	28	26	7	1	23	22	17	2
Retention	36	20	3	3	27	23	12	2

TABLE XV

HAVING AND USING PERSONAL TOWEL,
EXPERIMENTAL AND CONTROL GROUPS

Group and Time of Interview	No. Having Own Towel	Frequency of Use of Own Towel		
		Always	Usually	Seldom
Experimental ($N = 62$)				
Pre-study	37	22	15	0
Post-study	44	26	17	1
Retention	45	29	15	1
Control ($N = 64$)				
Pre-study	50	25	22	3
Post-study	49	24	23	2
Retention	47	28	18	1

TABLE XVI

HAVING AND USING PERSONAL WASHCLOTH,
EXPERIMENTAL AND CONTROL GROUPS

Group and Time of Interview	No. Having Own Washcloth	Frequency of Use of Own Washcloth		
		Always	Usually	Seldom
Experimental ($N = 62$)				
Pre-study	45	29	14	2
Post-study	47	32	13	2
Retention	44	34	7	3
Control ($N = 64$)				
Pre-study	54	41	9	4
Post-study	52	39	12	1
Retention	52	38	14	0

TABLE XVII

HAVING AND USING PERSONAL DRINKING GLASS,
EXPERIMENTAL AND CONTROL GROUPS

Group and Time of Interview	No. Having Own Glass	Frequency of Use of Own Glass		
		Always	Usually	Seldom
Experimental (N = 62)				
Pre-study	41	21	18	2
Post-study	45	20	22	3
Retention	43	24	15	4
Control (N = 64)				
Pre-study	34	15	13	6
Post-study	24	10	8	6
Retention	38	20	10	8

TABLE XVIII

"GIVING A BITE," OF FOOD BEING EATEN, TO ANOTHER PERSON,
EXPERIMENTAL AND CONTROL GROUPS

Group and Time of Interview	Frequency of "Giving a Bite"			
	Never	Seldom	Often	Very Often
Experimental (N = 62)				
Pre-study	10	31	15	6
Post-study	23	30	8	1
Retention	20	29	10	3
Control (N = 64)				
Pre-study	13	30	18	3
Post-study	14	33	15	2
Retention	14	38	10	2

TABLE XIX

"TAKING A BITE," OF FOOD BEING EATEN BY ANOTHER PERSON,
EXPERIMENTAL AND CONTROL GROUPS

Group and Time of Interview	Frequency of "Taking a Bite"			
	Never	Seldom	Often	Very Often
Experimental (N = 62)				
Pre-study	14	28	14	6
Post-study	22	32	7	1
Retention	24	28	9	1
Control (N = 64)				
Pre-study	18	28	16	2
Post-study	16	31	16	1
Retention	17	36	10	1

TABLE XX

FREQUENCY OF HAVING A CLEAN HANDKERCHIEF,
EXPERIMENTAL AND CONTROL GROUPS

Group and Time of Interview	Frequency of Having Clean Handkerchief		
	Daily	Almost Daily	Irregularly
Experimental (N = 62)			
Pre-study	25	24	13
Post-study	28	29	5
Retention	29	27	6
Control (N = 64)			
Pre-study	29	29	6
Post-study	25	30	9
Retention	25	29	10

share of control. Perhaps if the pupils had been older their influence in the home environment might have been greater; as it was, they were largely dominated by the authority of their parents and by the habits followed in their households.

ANALYSIS OF CHANGES IN BEHAVIOR WHEN ILL

Table XXI summarizes the changes which took place in the behavior of pupils who were ill. It is recognized that the data here are probably not perfectly objective. For example, the first sign of a communicable illness might not be discernible either to the patient or to his mother. But the fact that the experimental group consistently showed gains while the control group in most cases showed slight gains, no gain at all, or even losses, cannot be considered merely coincidental.

Here again it was found that limiting factors were in operation to minimize the changes which might have occurred. Some pupils were loath to remain at home at the first indication of a cold because they were afraid of falling behind in their school work, and so were in attendance even when they realized they should not have been. They were not unlike some adults in this respect. Others were not permitted by their parents to stay home, but were forced to come to school.

Other pupils in the experimental group did not have their

temperatures taken because they had no clinical thermometer in their home. Many of those who took patent medicines (which ranged all the way from aspirin for a sore throat to medications which were rubbed on the chest for chest colds, or stuffed up the nose for head colds) in the pre-study period continued to do so afterwards because they were convinced by the faith of their parents in these remedies that they would be cured by such treatment. Later, however, several changed their testimony to a point which made evident the fact that they were now seeking relief rather than a cure.

In many instances, too, the experimental pupils left matters to the judgment of their parents even when this was contrary to what they had learned in school.

TABLE XXI

BEHAVIORS OF PUPILS ABSENT FROM SCHOOL BECAUSE OF COMMUNICABLE ILLNESS,
EXPERIMENTAL AND CONTROL GROUPS

Behavior	Group	Pre-study			Post-study			%
		Yes	No	% Yes	Yes	No	% Yes	Gain
Stay home at first sign of illness	Experimental ...	12	14	46.2	19	11	63.3	17.1
	Control	15	14	51.7	13	16	44.8	−6.9
Go to bed immediately	Experimental ...	18	8	69.2	27	3	90.0	20.8
	Control	24	5	82.8	25	4	86.2	3.4
Remain in bed until well	Experimental ...	14	12	53.8	21	9	70.0	16.2
	Control	15	14	51.7	19	10	65.5	13.8
Have pulse rate taken	Experimental ...	4	22	15.4	8	22	26.6	11.2
	Control	7	22	24.1	6	23	20.7	−3.4
Have temperature taken	Experimental ...	12	14	46.2	22	8	73.3	27.1
	Control	14	15	49.3	15	14	51.7	2.4
Consulting a physician	Experimental ...	4	22	15.4	12	18	40.0	24.6
	Control	9	20	31.0	9	20	31.0	0.0
Having visitors	Experimental ...	13	13	50.0	12	18	40.0	10.0
	Control	12	17	41.4	10	19	34.5	6.9
Taking patent medicines	Experimental ...	21	5	80.7	19	11	63.3	17.4
	Control	23	6	79.3	20	9	69.0	10.3
Sterilization of eating utensils	Experimental ...	10	16	38.5	17	13	56.6	18.1
	Control	15	14	51.7	15	14	51.7	0.0
Sterilization of handkerchiefs	Experimental ...	17	9	69.2	27	3	90.0	20.8
	Control	22	7	75.9	22	7	75.9	0.0

SUMMARY

The following conclusions may be drawn from the data which have been presented:

1. The pupils in this experiment possessed a number of behaviors which may be considered detrimental to their health.

2. Study of communicable diseases by these pupils brought about changes in their undesirable behaviors.

3. The extent of these changes can be estimated by means of direct observations and interviews with the pupils.

4. Greater changes occur in the simpler behaviors than in those complicated by external factors.

OTHER EVIDENCE OF CHANGES IN BEHAVIOR

In addition to the data obtained by observations and interviews, there were other evidences of changes in overt behavior. Records of such evidence were kept during the progress of the experiment and for twelve weeks afterwards, or to the close of what has been referred to as the retention period.

All during the experiment and in later weeks pupils would volunteer unsolicited remarks about things which they were. now doing differently from the way they did them before their study of communicable diseases. These were tabulated and are given here in support of the argument that learning does affect behavior. Of the sixty-two pupils in the experimental group, a total of fifty-three made comments which seemed to be of significance in this study.

Eleven different pupils, five of them boys and six girls, had the following to say about putting their fingers in their mouths:

"Have you noticed that I don't put my fingers in my mouth so often?"

"I've been trying to remember not to put pencils, fingers, and such things in my mouth."

"I don't put nearly so many things in my mouth as I used to."

"I don't put things in my mouth, other than foods, as much as I used to."

"I don't run my fingers through my hair and then put them in my mouth like I used to."

"I try to remember to keep my fingers and other things away from my mouth, eyes, nose, and so on."

"I try not to put my fingers or any other objects in my mouth."

"I rarely ever put my fingers in my mouth any more."

"I'm trying not to put my fingers in my mouth."

"I don't put 'bobby pins' in my mouth any more."

"I don't put my pencil in my mouth any more ever."

Four pupils, three girls and a boy, offered the following information about their habit of fingernail-biting:

"I try not to bite my fingernails now."

"I do not bite my fingernails any more."

"I just don't bite my fingernails now."

"See, I've quit biting my fingernails."

One girl said: "Among other things, I've quit picking my nose." A boy remarked on his way out of class one day, "Now I use a clean handkerchief when I rub my eyes."

Thirteen pupils, seven girls and six boys, told the investigator that they were more careful about using their handkerchiefs when coughing or sneezing. Their remarks are listed:

"Now I always use a handkerchief when I cough or sneeze."

"I certainly use my hanky when coughing or sneezing a lot more than before we studied diseases."

"I tell my younger sister to use a handkerchief when she coughs. I myself am more particular about using a handkerchief when coughing or sneezing."

"I use a handkerchief most of the time now when I sneeze or cough."

"I try to always use a handkerchief when I sneeze or cough."

"I try to remember to use a handkerchief when I cough."

"I always use a handkerchief when I cough or sneeze now."

"I've learned that coughing or sneezing spreads germs, so now I always use my handkerchief."

"Now I always use a handkerchief when sneezing or coughing."

"You should see me use my handkerchief when I sneeze."

"When I see someone coughing without using a handkerchief I'm always reminded of what we learned in biology."

"I always use a handkerchief now, especially when I sneeze."

"I try to use my handkerchief when coughing or sneezing, no matter if I'm in the room alone."

"The other day I was riding on a bus and noticed that the man back of me kept coughing. That didn't used to bother me, but now it did, because he didn't use a handkerchief, so I changed my seat."

Several pupils also remarked that they were more careful about washing their hands frequently than they had been. They made the following comments:

"I didn't used to wash my hands at school very much before lunch as I do now."

"I wash my hands as much as possible before helping cook supper at home."

"Nowadays I wash my hands much more often before dinner."

"I always wash my hands before eating, when possible, except at school."

"Now I wash my hands before eating dinner until they are very clean."

"I make sure to wash my hands before all my meals now."

"I wash my hands much more often before dinner these days."

"Now I always wash my hands before dinner."

"I have washed my face and hands before eating after learning about communicable diseases."

"I wash my hands before eating more often than ever before."

"Now I always wash my hands before my meals."

Six pupils volunteered the information that they were more careful about washing their hands after having been to the lavatory. They said:

"I always now, if possible, wash my hands after going to the toilet. I never used to before studying about diseases."

"One thing I learned to do, that is to wash my hands after having been to the toilet."

"I didn't used to wash my hands after going to the toilet, at home or at school, but now I always do."

"Most every time after having been to the lavatory now I wash my hands."

"I wash my hands after going to the toilet after learning about communicable diseases."

"Now I always wash my hands after going to the bathroom."

Some pupils reported that they washed their hands more frequently at other times than those previously mentioned. Their testimony was:

"Since I saw what bacteria we carry on our hands, I always wash mine after playing or fooling around."

"After playing with my dog, I now make sure to always wash my hands."

"Those bacteria plates convinced me. Now I always wash my hands after playing with Pal. He's my dog."

"I always wash my hands after playing with the dog."

"I always wash my hands now after petting my pets."

"After washing my dog I now always wash me, too."

"I wash my hands much more often than I used to."

"Now I always remember to wash my hands after handling a dog or cat or other animal."

"It surprises me to see how often I find it necessary to wash my hands nowadays."

"I'm washing my hands much more often than I used to."

"I wash my hands a little more often than before."

Two girls and one boy were more careful about the cleanliness of the glasses out of which they drank. The boy said: "Now I always wash the glass out before drinking out of it if I think somebody else has used it." The girls said: "I don't drink from a glass used by another person at any time, whether in school, or at home, or any place," and "I always use my own drinking glass now."

A significant incident with bearing on this point transpired in one of the local drugstores which is popular with the high school student body. The investigator made it a point to spend some time there. On at least six different occasions he heard pupils from the experimental group ask for soft drinks in paper cups instead of glasses. To one of them the clerk once remarked: "You didn't used to be so particular." To this the pupil replied: "No, but I've been watching lately how those glasses are washed. I'll take my 'coke' in a paper cup, thank you." This exchange took place at the counter; the investigator was sitting at a booth so placed that he was not readily seen by pupils. At no time were any of the control pupils observed to be particular about the containers from which they drank.

Experimental pupils also volunteered the information that they were not so prone to "take a bite" or "give a bite" of food which was being eaten. Eleven of these were girls, two were boys. They had this to say about their change in this type of behavior:

"I used to take bites of candy, and give bites, but now I break a piece off. It's just as easy."

"I don't take a bite of things that others are eating any more."

"I used to take bites and give bites of food, but I very seldom do it any more."

"I still give bites of candy because other kids don't understand why they shouldn't, but I don't take bites as much as I used to."

"I don't give people a bite of candy any more. I break it off for them."

"I don't offer bites any more, and when they ask me I try to talk them out of it. I don't accept bites from other people as much, but I still do sometimes."

"I always used to give everybody a bite of candy, but now I don't. I advise other people to keep their candy and other food to themselves."

"I don't take a bite of cake or something as much as I did."

"I've been refusing bites of candy from other people, but I give them some of mine out of politeness."

"I still give a bite of candy to other people, but I really am trying to reform from this bad habit."

"I seldom give a bite, or seldom take a bite, any more."

"No, I don't take a bite or give a bite as much as usual."

"I don't give a bite or take one any more since I saw what bacteria are in the mouth."

Two boys and three girls mentioned that they were more careful about having a clean handkerchief than they had been. The boys said: "I can't use a dirty handkerchief any more. Now I always take a clean one every morning without being reminded by Mother," and "After seeing all the things for which I used my handkerchief I decided that I'd better have a clean one every day." One of the girls remarked that "I used to carry the same handkerchief in my purse for a week, but now I take a clean one every day if I've used the other at all." A second girl said: "Now I always remember to have a clean handkerchief with me," and the third, "I never realized before why I should have a clean handkerchief. Now that I do I always have one whether I think I'll need it or not."

Other reports of changes in behavior also came in voluntarily. Two girls said that they had occasionally borrowed lipsticks, but that they had stopped doing so. A boy said: "I really try to keep away from people who are coughing." Another boy offered this information: "I used to have a habit of spitting, but now I don't spit at all, anywhere." Another boy said that he tried to stay away from people who are sick "because I know now how easily diseases are transmitted." One boy said that he tried to get his mother to cover the sugar bowl after it had been used, "because of all the bacteria floating around in the air." This was an unexpected application of what he had learned in his study of communicable diseases.

One girl said that she was now careful to use only her own toothbrush, remarking that "It didn't used to make any difference to me which one I took, but it certainly does now, even if it is all in the family."

That the knowledge gained in their study of communicable diseases was probably being applied in a variety of places is indicated by a number of incidents. For example, one of the boys in the experimental group had been waiting at a water fountain in one of the school corridors for his turn to get a drink. When he was next in line he looked at the fountain, and then remarked to the instructor who had been standing close by: "I didn't used to notice it, but now I think these water fountains are a menace to health. Something ought to be done about it—the pressure is so low that you can't get a drink without putting your mouth right on the pipe where the water comes out. I've been watching, and that's what everybody is doing, and I just can't drink after that. I'm going to take it up with the student council at the next meeting."

Three weeks after the study of the unit on diseases had ended, one of the experimental pupils came to the instructor with the following request: "May I borrow one of those 'Communicable Disease' booklets to take home? My kid sister has been exposed to German measles, and Mother wants to know how long the incubation period is, and when the disease is communicable, so that if there is any danger of my getting it I can be moved to another house before it gets me, too." Another girl had been absent from school three days; when she returned to class she reported that she had had a sore throat, and remarked, "But, boy, was I really careful not to let it spread in the family!"

Two pupils, a boy and a girl, became sufficiently concerned about their immunity to smallpox to report to the investigator that they had tried to find out when they had been vaccinated. The boy, apparently from a family with a low income, asked where and by whom he might be vaccinated without charge. "My mother doesn't remember when I was last vaccinated," he said, "so I told her that the best thing to do was to be vaccinated again." After having been given the information, he later proudly displayed his scar. The girl made no inquiries; she merely reported to class one day with the comment that "No one at home seemed to know when I had been vaccinated, so I argued until Dad took me to the doctor for vaccination to make sure I was immune."

It is possible that there might have been other such instances to report were it not for the fact that two years before the beginning of this study the local Board of Education had passed legislation requiring all pupils to show evidence of recent vaccination or else to be immunized, unless parents swore out an affidavit testifying that they objected to the procedure on religious or other grounds.

Upon having acquired information concerning communicable diseases, many of the experimental pupils told about how they had been spreading their newly acquired knowledge at home and in other places. A list of their voluntary contributions to the investigator follows:

"I always ask people I know, if they are coughing, if they would use a handkerchief."

"I have fun giving advice to other people about what they should do when coughing or sneezing."

"My mother gets mad when I start harping about not using a handkerchief when my brother or sister cough."

"I don't suppose I do things much differently even now, but I do tell other people what not to do."

"I always advise other people what to do when they are coughing, or sneezing."

"I advised my cousin to wash his hands after going to the toilet, and to use his handkerchief when he coughs."

"You should hear me tell people, especially my mother, about washing their hands after petting the dog."

"I sure do tell people at home how to protect their health!"

"When I see other people doing the wrong thing I always try to educate them now."

"I've been advising all my friends what they can do to stay healthy."

"When I tell other people what they should do I can prove that I'm right, now. That makes them pay attention to me."

"I've been teaching my small sister about using her handkerchief, bacteria, and all that stuff. I also try to keep her away from small children and babies when she has a cold."

"People don't like to be told things, do they? I've been telling some of my friends what they shouldn't do, and they don't listen much."

"I've been trying to correct the whole family to better health habits."

"Since I am much more informed about communicable diseases, I tell others what I have learned."

"Some friends of mine dropped some food on the floor. They picked it up and were going to eat it, but I told them not to."

"I almost always make my little sister wash her hands before eating. If I don't, someone else does. My mother always used to do this, but now that I know how important clean hands are I do it."

"I've been telling my younger brother not to do certain things, but I guess he's too young to understand."

"I tell my father and mother not to cough at the dinner table. They use their hands over their mouth when they do, but I showed them that wasn't enough."

"I tell everybody in the house what they are doing wrong until they are about ready to throw me out."

"I bawl out my family when they sneeze or cough and don't do anything about it."

"I often tell others that they should keep their fingers away from their mouth because of the bacteria on their hands."

"I always tell people not to do different things if they happen to be doing them."

"I tell my mother, sister, and brother to cover their mouth if they cough or sneeze."

"I tell my younger sister to use a handkerchief when she coughs."

The investigator happened to be in the lavatory in which there were a number of boys at the time, some of them from the classes involved in this experiment. Two boys, one from each of the experimental classes, were washing their hands. One of them remarked to the investigator about the other: "His class must be studying communicable diseases, too. He never used to wash his hands in here before."

FACTORS TENDING TO RETARD CHANGES IN OVERT BEHAVIOR

There is some reason to believe that there are factors which tend to retard changes in overt behavior which otherwise might occur. Nine different pupils from the experimental group voluntarily related instances of conflict between what their parents or teachers believed and what was learned in the classroom. No doubt there were other such cases which pupils did not mention.

The information volunteered by the pupils is given below:

A boy said: "I can't stay home when I have a cold. My Dad always gets sore when I do. He doesn't think a cold should keep anyone away from his work."

A girl told the investigator one day: "You can't stay home from school just because of a cold. There's too much home work to be done, and then you get 'way behind. The teachers want you to make it all up the day after you come back, and that's too hard."

Another girl had this to say: "I am not allowed to stay home from school unless I am so sick I can't get out of bed. My French teacher says: 'Were you so sick you couldn't come to school? My goodness, I never let a little thing like a cold prevent me from doing my work!'"

Still another girl, speaking of a different teacher, said: "Oh, I didn't dare stay home. I just didn't dare miss any work; my French marks are so low I'd flunk if I did."

One of the boys reported that he had asked his sister to stop coughing at the dinner table, since she was not using her handkerchief. He then related what he had learned in school about the transmission of respiratory diseases by droplet infection. "My father said: 'Just listen to the little doctor.' My father always makes fun of me when I tell at home what I learned in school."

"We get into all sorts of arguments at home about patent medicines," remarked a girl one day. "That's all we talk about at the dinner table. I had a cold, and my mother wanted me to take ————, but I wouldn't because I can't see how anything rubbed on your chest would do an infection in the bronchial tubes any good. My brother, who is taking a pre-medical course at Syracuse, agreed with me and didn't want me to take the stuff, either, but finally Father made me."

A somewhat similar reaction came from another pupil, a girl. She said: "We were talking about communicable diseases at home last night. My dad says that there are plenty of good cures for a cold on the market. He says only Christian Scientists don't believe that."

Slightly different in tone was the following reaction, reported by a boy: "My dad says that what we said in class the other day about patent medicines and advertising is bad for business and un-American. He doesn't think we should be so radical."

One further bit of evidence must be submitted. This is the case of a boy from what might be considered a good family. His father is a research engineer; his mother, also a college graduate, is active in community affairs. Shortly after the last of the data presented here had been gathered, the boy was absent from school for ten days. When he returned he had this to relate: "I had the measles. My mother brought my sister into my room when I had them so she could get them from me. My mother wanted her to get them, because Sis has been quarantined from school five times on account of contact with measles. Mother thought that if she got them and got it over with, she wouldn't get quarantined again and wouldn't have to be out of school so much. Our doctor didn't advise it, but when Mother told him the circumstances he thought it would be a good idea."

These anecdotes would seem to indicate, then, that in some cases at least, desirable changes in behavior are discouraged by influences outside the school. The influence of parents on children is no doubt sufficiently great to have such an effect on the learner. The teacher, however, has the benefit of medical authority on his side, and this does make an impression on the child. Children might be skeptical of what they are learning if they thought it was merely the belief and opinion of the instructor, but they seem to accept the learning materials when they are shown that these are derived from recognized authorities. They then quote these authorities to their parents, according to their reports to the investigator, and in some instances take home the "Communicable Disease" booklet issued by the government to prove their point.

There may be some significance in the fact that while the venereal diseases received at least as much attention in the unit as any others, or perhaps even somewhat more because of the intense interest of the learners in them, not one parent raised any objection. The fathers of two boys and the mother of another, chancing to meet the investigator, lauded this phase of the work, so that it is apparent that at least some of the children discussed it at home.

It is also interesting to note that the parents of seven pupils were reported by their children, pupils involved in the experiment, to have read the learning materials used in the study.

LEARNING MATERIALS CONTRIBUTING
TO BEHAVIOR CHANGES

It may be of some use to indicate which of the learning materials outlined in Chapter III seemed to be of greatest influence on the changes in behavior. It will be seen that some of the material contributed directly to whatever changes may have taken place. For the sake of convenience these will be reviewed from the assignment schedule.

Assignment 2 was meant to give the learner an overview of the work, and to lead him to a realization of the importance of a knowledge of the communicable diseases. Assignment 3 was devoted to a definition of the problem; as a result of it, the pupil was led to identify himself with it.

In the fourth and fifth assignments, the size, weight, distribution, rate of reproduction, and other problems were considered. A realization of the microscopic nature of pathogens was deemed necessary in order to give the pupil an understanding of the ease with which they can be conveyed. For example, it was less difficult for the pupil to understand how a pathogen may travel through the air as the result of a cough or sneeze if he had some idea of its weight. The pupil activity with the culture plates demonstrated the omnipresence of microorganisms in a way which, judging from the reactions in class, made a deep impression. Assignments 6 and 7 attempted something of a similar nature with Protozoa and filtrable viruses.

Assignment 8, dealing with methods of transmission of diseases, developed the importance of using a handkerchief when coughing or sneezing, and conveyance of microorganisms by other means, such as drinking glasses, towels, food being shared by two persons, and so forth. In the tenth assignment attention was given to the periods of communicability of the diseases; this was intended to lead the learner to an appreciation of the need for remaining at home when ill with a communicable disease, since many of them are most communicable in their early stages.

Assignments 12 to 16, inclusive, dealt specifically with each of the fifteen diseases. The symptoms, etiological agents, sources of infection, modes of transmission, periods of communicability, methods of immunization and prevention were considered. In each instance the pertinent behavior changes were stressed. In the seventeenth assignment the means by which pathogens enter the body were studied. In a previous assignment pupils learned that pathogens are present everywhere; here they learned that many of them enter the body through the mouth; from this the pupils were able to draw their own conclusions and did so. Vaccination and immunization were discussed in the twentieth assignment.

The importance of prompt medical attention and measures to be taken at home were discussed in the twenty-first assignment. This was followed by a consideration of the need for isolation in some of the diseases, and the need for remaining in bed until recovery. The importance of immunization as a general measure was emphasized again in the twenty-third assignment, and in the next one concurrent disinfection was studied, with a re-emphasis on personal cleanliness.

Of the thirty periods used in the study, change in behavior entered into consideration during seventeen of them. The instructor was careful never to issue directives on these changes; in practicallly every case the need for changes was first mentioned by the pupils themselves. As a result, and because some of the pupils were not easily convinced by their classmates, it sometimes became necessary to resort to experimentation and demonstration. For example, a boy doubted that there could be many bacteria on his pencil. A culture plate was streaked and incubated together with a control plate. The results were convincing enough to cause the boy to change his behavior.

It may be pertinent to mention here that much of the instruction was directed at changes in behavior. In other words, specific outcomes were sought, and, as has been shown, achieved. Not all the work was aimed at the changes in behavior which were attained, but a large proportion of it dealt with the need for the changes. The investigator feels that this specificity of purpose is necessary for achieving any desired educational outcome.

INTERCORRELATIONS OF THE EXPERIMENTAL FACTORS

Since changes in overt behavior resulting from educational experiences have not been widely explored, a consideration of some of the relationships of the experimental factors is pertinent. Tables XXII–XXV present some of the intercorrelations obtained.

Table XXII shows the relationship between intelligence quotient and scores made on the information test, observed behavior, Interview A, and Interview B.

Lindquist[1] states that to be significantly different from zero,

---

[1] Lindquist, E. F., *Statistical Analysis in Educational Research,* pp. 210–213. Houghton, Mifflin Co., Boston, 1940.

TABLE XXII

Correlations Between Intelligence Quotient[1] and Scores Made
on Information Test,[2] Observed Behaviors,[3] Interview A,
and Interview B[4] in the Pre-study, Post-
study, and Retention Periods

Group	Information Test	Observed Behavior	Interview A	Interview B
Experimental				
Pre-study	.64	.33	.20	.03
Post-study	.56	.002	.12	..
Retention	.51	.19	.14	.12
Control				
Pre-study	.41	−.01	.32	.21
Post-study	.41	−.05	.14	..
Retention	.39	−.05	.34	.18

[1] As determined by Otis Self-Administering Test.
[2] Form A, in pre-study period and retention period; Form B in post-study period.
[3] Based on scores made in biology class observations.
[4] Based on: pre-study, 26 experimental pupils with mean I.Q. of 109.52, SD 10.71; 29 control pupils, mean I.Q. 110.35, SD 10.63. Post-study, 30 experimental pupils, mean I.Q. 108.06, SD 17.08; 30 control pupils, mean I.Q. 109.60, SD 10.55.

a correlation coefficient based on sixty scores must be at least .330 at the 1 per cent level. Thus, the only experimental group coefficients in Table XXII which show much significance are those between the intelligence scores and scores on the information tests, and the pre-study observed behavior scores. For the control group, numbering sixty-four cases, a coefficient is significantly different from zero at the 1 per cent level if it is .317 or greater. This criterion is met in the correlations between intelligence scores and the information test, and is just barely met on the pre-study and retention period Interview A scores.

The other coefficients reported in Table XXII are all so low that they cannot be considered as differing significantly from zero at either the 5 per cent or the 1 per cent levels. It may be judged from them that there is probably no real correlation between intelligence quotients as obtained by the usual tests and the behaviors studied in this investigation. This substantiates the claim that there is need for making changes in behavior an objective of education, since it apparently cannot be assumed that intelligence alone predisposes the learner to what might be considered intelligent behavior.

Table XXIII indicates, furthermore, that there was no statistically significant correlation between scores made on the information tests and behavior. It is true, however, that at the 5 per cent level of significance for the correlation between the information test scores and Interview B the coefficient need be only .367 for twenty-nine cases and .361 for thirty cases; two of the coefficients reported are .41.

TABLE XXIII

CORRELATIONS BETWEEN SCORES MADE ON THE INFORMATION TESTS AND OBSERVED BEHAVIOR,[1] INTERVIEW A, AND INTERVIEW B[2]

Group	Observed Behavior	Interview A	Interview B
Experimental			
Pre-study	.003	.18	.31
Post-study	.04	.17	..
Retention	.14	.002	.41
Control			
Pre-study	.08	.21	.41
Post-study	.004	.13	..
Retention	−.09	.17	.23

[1] Based on observations made in biology classes.
[2] Based on: pre-study, 26 experimental pupils, mean information test score 77.65, SD 14.19; 29 control pupils, mean information test score 80.07, SD 13.93. Post-study, 30 experimental pupils, mean information test score 98.10, SD 9.22; 30 control pupils, mean information test score 82.67, SD 12.08.

Here is evidence that acquisition of information has no particular correlation with changes in behavior, which emphasizes the previously made statement that a paper-and-pencil test on behavior would probably only indicate that the pupil knows what to do, not that he actually does it. Nor can a teacher assume that pupils automatically change their behavior simply because they possess facts which they previously had not known. It may be suggested here that further studies of this kind may show that the development of proper attitudes has an important bearing on behavior changes that are desired.

Moreover, Table XXIV indicates that there is little, if any, relationship among the various phases of behavior studied.

TABLE XXIV

CORRELATIONS BETWEEN OBSERVED BEHAVIOR[1] SCORES AND SCORES
MADE ON INTERVIEW A AND INTERVIEW B[2]

Group	Interview A	Interview B
Experimental		
Pre-study	.25	−.01
Post-study	−.09	..
Retention	−.05	−.07
Control		
Pre-study	−.18	−.16
Post-study	−.11	..
Retention	−.13	.01

[1] Based on scores made in biology classes.
[2] Based on: pre-study, 26 experimental pupils, mean observed behavior score 17.65, SD 15.96; 29 control pupils, mean observed behavior score 18.03, SD 12.02. Post-study, 30 experimental pupils, mean observed behavior score 3.87, SD 2.77; 30 control pupils, mean observed behavior score 20.07, SD 10.94.

Thus, on the basis of this evidence, it cannot be assumed that a pupil who makes a high score in the observed behaviors, let us say, will do as well on Interview A or Interview B. These latter behaviors, therefore, must be taken into consideration and not simply taken for granted.

TABLE XXV

CORRELATIONS BETWEEN SCORES MADE IN INTERVIEW A AND
INTERVIEW B

Period	Group	
	Experimental	Control
Pre-study	.58	.30
Post-study	.38	.48

The correlations given in Table XXV are higher than others reported, but it must be remembered that they are based on a smaller number of pupils. In the pre-study experimental group there were twenty-six pupils whose mean Interview A score was

64.42, with a standard deviation of 17.48; the control group consisted of twenty-nine pupils whose mean Interview A score was 73.42, with a standard deviation of 19.21. In the post-study experimental group there were thirty pupils with a mean score of 76.90, and a standard deviation of 14.64; the thirty control pupils this time had a mean Interview A score of 70.10 and a standard deviation of 13.56.

Whether or not these correlation coefficients are significant again may be tested by comparison with Lindquist's[2] table giving the values of significant coefficients at the 5 per cent and the 1 per cent levels. A coefficient based on twenty-nine scores is significant at the 5 per cent level if it is .367 or higher, and at the 1 per cent level if it is .471 or higher. For thirty scores, the 5 per cent level of significance is .361, while the 1 per cent level calls for a coefficient of .463. For twenty-six cases, the coefficient must be .388 at the 5 per cent level and .496 at the 1 per cent level.

The low intercorrelations among the scores made on the tests, observed behaviors, Interview A, and Interview B indicate also that each of these measures different attributes. It is of interest to note that in many instances the post-study and retention correlations are lower than those derived for the pre-study data, despite the fact that the experimental group showed gains in each of the variables.

Pupils apparently do not integrate their experiences equally, nor do they progress equally in a given direction. Perhaps more work in this area by the pupils would eventually bring them all to approximately the same point. It is also possible that environmental influences outside the classroom exert an effect on the pupil which cannot be overcome in a few weeks.

SUMMARY

1. There seems to be some correlation between intelligence quotient and what pupils know about communicable diseases as determined by the tests used, but little, if any, correlation between intelligence quotient and behaviors as here defined.

2. There is no significant correlation between information

[2] Lindquist, E. F., *op. cit.*

about communicable diseases and pupil behavior, both as defined in this study.

3. There is no significant correlation among the three phases of overt behavior studied. There is less after six weeks of study than before.

4. While the data would seem to indicate that there is some correlation between behavior as determined by Interviews A and B, this was necessarily based on a small number of pupils and so cannot be held to be conclusive.

TABLE XXVI

SIGNIFICANCE OF GAINS MADE IN THE POST-STUDY AND RETENTION
SCORES OVER PRE-STUDY SCORES BY THE EXPERIMENTAL
AND CONTROL GROUPS

Score	Group	Gains in Post-study Over Pre-study Means			Gains in Retention Over Pre-study Means		
		$\overline{G}$*	$\sigma_{\overline{G}}$*	$\overline{G}/\sigma_{\overline{G}}$*	$\overline{G}$	$\sigma_{\overline{G}}$	$\overline{G}/\sigma_{\overline{G}}$
Information Test	Experimental ...	43.45	1.55	28.03	24.60	1.85	13.30
	Control	4.94	0.86	5.74	2.52	0.55	4.54
Observed Behaviors, Biology	Experimental ...	14.78	1.77	8.37	14.61	1.70	8.59
	Control	−2.46	0.81	3.04	−3.14	0.62	5.06
Observed Behaviors, English	Experimental ...	15.93	2.13	7.46	15.53	2.17	7.17
	Control	−0.28	0.77	0.36	0.09	0.80	0.11
Interview A	Experimental ...	10.26	1.14	9.00	9.66	1.28	7.55
	Control	−1.56	0.87	1.79	1.32	−.42	3.14
Interview B	Experimental ...	20.41	3.33	6.13			
	Control	−1.90	3.31	0.57			

* $\overline{G}$ = mean gain; $\sigma_{\overline{G}}$ = standard error; $\overline{G}/\sigma_{\overline{G}}$ = ratio mean gain to standard error. Reliability of mean gain: a ratio of 3 is considered virtual certainty, (99.9 chances in 100 that the true difference is greater than zero) according to Garrett, H. E., *Statistics in Psychology and Education*, p. 213. Longmans, Green and Co., 1937.

Ratio:	.10	.35	.55	1.80	3.00
Chances in 100	54	64	71	96	99.9

SIGNIFICANCE OF THE REPORTED GAINS

Table XXVI shows the gains made by both the experimental and the control groups in the four experimental variables. It will be seen that the experimental group made very significant gains in all instances, and that very significant portions of the gains were retained for at least three months, until the retention period data were obtained.

Since the control group made much smaller gains, and since the significance of these gains was not nearly so high, it may be assumed that the gains of the experimental group could not have been due, in the case of the information test, to the practice effect of taking the test three times.

It will be seen that the gains in the observed behaviors were retained in English classes as well as in the biology classes, indicating that the changes which took place were carried over to situations away from the scene of instruction. Some of the anecdotal material reported tends to bear out this impression.

Chapter VII

SUMMARY

THIS investigation was undertaken because of the author's conviction that no evaluation of pupil progress resulting from educational experiences is complete unless some data on changes in overt behavior are obtained and analyzed. That this conviction is shared by others was pointed out in Chapter I.

In undertaking to determine whether or not educational experiences can bring about desirable behavior changes, it was decided to work in the area of Communicable Diseases, which seemed to present excellent opportunity for such an investigation, since some of the aspects of behavior involved in the control of such diseases could be observed directly in the classroom. Other pertinent aspects were studied by means of interviews.

An exploration of the area indicated that fifteen communicable diseases either were so common that some of them had been experienced by most of the children and were persistent human problems in this country, or were under control only because measures could be and had been taken to reduce their prevalence. Continued education of the public in these latter diseases was deemed necessary for their continued control. When the diseases had been chosen, a unit of learning materials was prepared as study material for the experimental pupils, supplemented by a wide variety of textbooks, pamphlets, government bulletins, audio-visual aids, and laboratory experiences.

On the basis of these learning materials, two forms of an information test were prepared. These were submitted for validation to a group of persons more competent than laymen in this area; they were then given to a group of tenth-grade pupils for determination of reliability.

The investigated behaviors were likewise submitted to a

group who passed on their validity in a study such as this. The observations were shown to be reliable when the scores of pupils, as determined by two observers working simultaneously, were shown to have a high coefficient of reliability. The reliability of the interviews was also found to be high; Interview B reliability was high when based on two interviews with a pupil about the same absence due to illness.

The tests were given, and the observations and interviews were carried out, in a pre-study period, following which the experimental group studied the prepared learning materials while the control group studied a unit not closely related. After six weeks both groups were given the second form of the test, and the observations and interviews were repeated; all was repeated again twelve weeks later.

Several conclusions may be drawn from the data. These are:

1. The experimental group made much larger gains than the control group on the information test. A considerable portion of these gains was lost in twelve weeks, but the mean of the experimental group scores was still much higher than the mean of the control group.

2. Although the observed behavior mean scores of the two groups were very similar at the outset of the experiment, the experimental group made great gains which were not matched by the control group. Moreover, the changes represented by these gains were maintained with but a slight loss for twelve weeks after the close of the learning period, indicating a degree of permanence in the changes.

3. In the behaviors described as Interview A, the experimental group again made and retained changes which were not matched by the control group. This was also true of the behaviors listed under Interview B.

4. All of the gains made by the experimental group were found to have high statistical significance.

5. The correlation between the intelligence quotients of the pupils and their scores on the information test was found to be significant; there was little if any significant correlation, however, between intelligence and the behaviors studied.

6. There was no significant correlation between scores made on the information test and the various behaviors. Correlation between the observed behaviors and those determined by interviews was not found to be significant statistically. There was a significant degree of correlation between Interview A and B for the experimental group and in one instance for the control group.

7. Since the two groups were much alike at the beginning of the experiment, and since the control group could not match the gains shown by the experimental pupils, it may be assumed that the changes shown here were due to the experiences provided in the classroom.

8. Since much of the learning was directed specifically at the desired changes, there is reason to think that this specificity may have been a factor in bringing about the desired results.

9. It has been demonstrated that changes in behavior can be brought about as a result of learning experiences, that such changes can be studied and evaluated in the classroom and school, and that this may be done by using known techniques.

Perhaps the ultimate test of the worth-whileness of bringing about the changes in behavior studied here would be a comparison of the health records of the two groups of pupils for a period of years following their work on communicable diseases. For example, the rates of absence from school because of communicable illness in the two groups might yield illuminating data.

The techniques used in this investigation might be used in others. Since there was found to be no significant correlation between gains in information and changes in behavior, it may be suggested that other factors are in operation. It is quite possible that changes in attitudes ought to be studied in this connection.

Finally, the procedures used here might be useful in evaluating the effects of learning in other areas of the biological sciences. Bingham[1] explored the effect of learning on certain

---

[1] Bingham, N. E., *Teaching Nutrition in Biology Classes.* Bureau of Publications, Teachers College, Columbia University, New York, 1939.

attitudes toward food, and on the ability of the learner to apply the principles learned to the interpretation of food advertising. This could well be extended to determine by direct observations in the school cafeteria whether or not the changes in attitudes were accompanied by changes in the kinds of food pupils bought; by interview it might be possible to determine whether or not the home diet was affected.

Bibliography

BOOKS—GENERAL

BROADHURST, JEAN and GIVENS, L. I. *Microbiology Applied to Nursing.* J. B. Lippincott Company, Philadelphia, 1937.

CALKINS, G. N. *The Biology of the Protozoa.* Lea and Febiger, Philadelphia, 1933.

FITZPATRICK, F. L. *The Control of Organisms.* Bureau of Publications, Teachers College, Columbia University, New York, 1940.

GARRETT, H. E. *Statistics in Psychology and Education.* Longmans, Green and Company, New York, 1937.

JORDAN, E. O. *General Bacteriology.* W. B. Saunders Company, Philadelphia, 1936.

LINDQUIST, E. F. *Statistical Analysis in Educational Research.* Houghton Mifflin Company, Boston, 1940.

MARTIN, E. G. *The Human Body.* Henry Holt and Company, New York, 1928.

MEYR, B. B. *Your Germs and Mine.* Doubleday, Doran and Company, Garden City, N. Y., 1934.

MILLER, D. F. and BLAYDES, G. W. *Methods and Materials for Teaching Biological Sciences.* McGraw-Hill Book Company, New York, 1938.

PARK, W. H., WILLIAMS, ANNA W., and KRUMWIEDE, CHARLES. *Pathogenic Microorganisms.* Lea and Febiger, Philadelphia, 1933.

PARRAN, T. *Shadow on the Land—Syphilis.* Reynal and Hitchcock, New York, 1937.

PETERS, C. C. and VAN VOORHIS, W. R. *Statistical Procedures and Their Mathematical Bases.* McGraw-Hill Book Company, New York, 1940.

Report of a Committee on the Function of Science in General Education. *Science in General Education.* D. Appleton-Century Company, New York, 1937.

ROSENAU, M. J. *Preventive Medicine and Hygiene.* D. Appleton-Century Company, New York, 1935.

The Technical Staff, Board of Examinations, University of Chicago. *Manual of Examination Methods.* University of Chicago Bookstore, Chicago, 1937. Second Edition.

THURSTONE, L. L. *The Reliability and Validity of Tests.* Edwards Brothers, Inc., Ann Arbor, Mich., 1939.

PERIODICALS

TYLER, R. W. "Techniques Evaluating Behavior." *Educational Research Bulletin* (Ohio State University), January 17, 1934, pp. 1–11.

UNITED STATES PUBLIC HEALTH SERVICE. *The Notifiable Diseases, Prevalence in States.* Reprint No. 426 (1916); Reprint No. 505 (1917); Reprint No. 551 (1918); Reprint No. 643 (1919); Reprint No. 681 (1920); Reprint No. 791 (1921); Reprint No. 879 (1922); Reprint No. 974 (1923); Reprint No. 1056 (1924); Reprint No. 1132 (1925); all reprints from the Public Health Reports. Government Printing Office, Washington, D. C.

UNITED STATES PUBLIC HEALTH SERVICE. *The Notifiable Diseases, Prevalence in States.* Supplement No. 67 (1926); Supplement No. 73 (1927); Supplement No. 79 (1928); Supplement No. 88 (1929); Supplement No. 104 (1930); Supplement No. 105 (1931); Supplement No. 109 (1932); Supplement No. 112 (1933); Supplement No. 117 (1934); Supplement No. 119 (1935); Supplement No. 134 (1936); Supplement No. 147 (1937); Supplement No. 160 (1938); Supplement No. 163 (1939); all supplements to the Public Health Reports. Government Printing Office, Washington, D. C.

UNITED STATES PUBLIC HEALTH SERVICE. *Public Health Reports.* "Relative Rank of Important Causes of Sickness and Death." Volume 51, No. 29, pp. 947–969, July 17, 1936. Government Printing Office, Washington, D. C.

UNITED STATES PUBLIC HEALTH SERVICE. "Sickness Incidence Among a Group of School Children." *Public Health Reports,* Vol. 40, No. 9, February 27, 1925. Government Printing Office, Washington, D. C.

UNITED STATES PUBLIC HEALTH SERVICE. *Laws and Regulations Relating to Morbidity Reporting* (Prepared by William Fowler). Supplement No. 100 to the Public Health Reports. Government Printing Office, Washington, D. C., 1933.

UNITED STATES PUBLIC HEALTH SERVICE. *The Control of Communicable Diseases* (Prepared by Haven Emerson, chairman of committee, and others). Reprint No. 1697 from the Public Health Reports, Vol. 50, No. 32, August 9, 1935. Government Printing Office, Washington, D. C.

THESES

BINGHAM, N. E. *Teaching Nutrition in Biology Classes.* Bureau of Publications, Teachers College, Columbia University, New York, 1939.

LATON, ANITA D. *The Psychology of Learning Applied to Health Education Through Biology.* Bureau of Publications, Teachers College, Columbia University, New York, 1929.

STATE AND LOCAL PUBLICATIONS

DEPARTMENT OF HEALTH, State of New Jersey. *Health and Vital Statistics, together with Extracts from Certain Other Statutes Relating to*

Public Health. Title 26, Circular 210, August, 1938. Department of Health, Trenton, New Jersey.

DEPARTMENT OF HEALTH, State of New Jersey. *Food and Drug Laws*. Circular 211, July, 1938. Department of Health, Trenton, New Jersey.

DEPARTMENT OF HEALTH, State of New Jersey. *Revised Statutes Relating to Waters, Water Supplies, and Sewerage Systems*. Circular 213, August, 1938. Department of Health, Trenton, New Jersey.

DEPARTMENT OF HEALTH, Millburn Township, New Jersey. *Revised Sanitary Code for Millburn Township*. Department of Health, Millburn, New Jersey.

MONOGRAPHS AND REPORTS

BIGELOW, KARL W. and others. *Report of a Committee Appointed to Consider a Proposal for an Enlarged Program of Work in the Field of General Education at Teachers College, Columbia University*. Unpublished. April, 1938.

LATON, ANITA D. and PILLEY, J. G. *Scientific Method*. Teachers College, Columbia University, New York, 1938.

LATON, ANITA D. and others. *Life Span*. Teachers College, Columbia University, New York, 1938.

MANWELL, E. A. *Physiological Exchange of Materials and Energy*. Bureau of Educational Research in Science, Teachers College, Columbia University, New York, 1938. (Mimeographed)

NATIONAL SOCIETY FOR THE STUDY OF EDUCATION. *Thirty-first Year Book*, Part I. Public School Publishing Company, Bloomington, Illinois, 1932.

RICHTER, MARION, URBAN, JOHN, and FITZPATRICK, F. L. *Educational Implications of Our Knowledge Concerning the Communicable Diseases*. Bureau of Educational Research in Science, Teachers College, Columbia University, New York, 1940. (Mimeographed)

UNITED STATES BUREAU OF EDUCATION. *Cardinal Principles of Secondary Education*. Bulletin No. 35, 1918. Government Printing Office, Washington, D. C.

UNITED STATES PUBLIC HEALTH SERVICE. *The Communicable Diseases*. (Prepared by A. M. Stimson, M.D.) Miscellaneous Publication No. 30. Government Printing Office, Washington, D. C.

Appendix

THE INFORMATION TESTS

FORM A

Name---------------------Grade--------Home Room--------Class------

Some of the following statements are true and some are false. Mark the true statements with the letter T, and the false statements with an O.

---O--- 1. Bacteria are microscopic animals.

---O--- 2. Bacteria reproduce by forming spores.

---T--- 3. Bacteria may reproduce once each hour.

---O--- 4. Diphtheria antitoxin is developed in pigs.

---O--- 5. Red corpuscles destroy disease organisms.

---T--- 6. Spirochetes have powers of locomotion.

---O--- 7. Mucus is a strong bactericide.

---T--- 8. Syphilis organisms can penetrate through mucous membranes.

---O--- 9. Bacteria contain chlorophyll.

---T--- 10. Tularemia may be contracted by handling the meat of wild rabbits.

---T--- 11. Cocci are spherical bacteria.

---T--- 12. Ciliary action sweeps small foreign particles out of the respiratory organs.

---T--- 13. Bacteria reproduce asexually.

---O--- 14. Diphtheria antitoxin contains red corpuscles.

---T--- 15. Rocky Mountain spotted fever is transmitted by ticks.

---O--- 16. Bacteria have well-developed nuclei.

---O--- 17. Jenner discovered a method for immunizing against diphtheria.

---O--- 18. Wassermann discovered a test for tuberculosis.

---T--- 19. Disinfection is the process of destroying bacteria with chemicals.

---O--- 20. Tuberculosis is a hereditary disease.

---T--- 21. Mosquitoes may be reduced in numbers by pouring oil on the water in which their larvae are found.

---T--- 22. Quinine is a drug useful in the treatment of malaria.

---O--- 23. Children can inherit syphilis from their parents.

---O--- 24. Houseflies are best controlled by "swatting" them.

97

___T___ 25. Lockjaw is caused by a bacterium commonly found in the soil.

___T___ 26. The brain tissue is damaged in the late stages of syphilis.

___T___ 27. Diphtheria could be practically eliminated by immunizing all non-immune children.

___O___ 28. Leprosy is caused by a worm-like parasite.

___T___ 29. Rabies is a disease of the nervous system.

___O___ 30. Athlete's foot is caused by an animal parasite.

___O___ 31. Cattle tuberculois organisms cause lung tuberculosis in man.

___O___ 32. The normal human body temperature is 88.4° F.

___O___ 33. Bacteria vary in length from one-fifth to one one-hundredth of an inch.

___O___ 34. Spherical bacteria move by means of flagella.

___T___ 35. Some Protozoa form cysts under unfavorable environmental conditions.

___T___ 36. Bacteria multiply rapidly in milk at room temperature.

___T___ 37. Nose mucus prevents some germs from being taken into the lungs.

___O___ 38. Pasteurization kills all microorganisms in milk.

___O___ 39. Babies born to mothers who have had diphtheria are immune to that disease for life.

___T___ 40. Oysters from sewage-contaminated water may transmit typhoid fever.

___T___ 41. Filtrable viruses may be grown in the laboratory.

___O___ 42. Malaria mosquitoes lay their eggs in rapidly flowing water.

___T___ 43. Syphilis is said to cause about 15 per cent of all blindness in the United States.

___O___ 44. Sanitary sewage disposal is essential for the control of measles.

___T___ 45. An object or substance is said to be sterile when it contains no living microorganisms.

___T___ 46. Some bacterial spores can survive boiling water temperatures.

___T___ 47. White corpuscles destroy disease organisms in the body.

___T___ 48. Tuberculosis is sometimes a disease of the bones.

___O___ 49. Hay fever is caused by bacteria.

___T___ 50. Children six months old may be safely immunized against diphtheria.

___O___ 51. Smallpox is a commoner disease in the United States today than it was one hundred years ago.

___T___ 52. Many kinds of disease germs enter the body through the mouth.

___O___ 53. Children should be encouraged to contract communicable diseases in order that they may develop immunity to them.

___T___ 54. Prolonged chilling tends to make a person more susceptible to diseases of the respiratory system.

___T___ 55. Children living with persons who have tuberculosis are likely to contract the disease.

___O___ 56. Colds are thought to be caused by bacteria.

___T___ 57. Some germs cause diseases by destroying body tissues.

___O___ 58. Good physical condition is a guarantee against contracting communicable diseases.

___O___ 59. "Isolation" means the segregation of persons who have been exposed to a communicable disease.

___O___ 60. Patent medicines which cure some of the communicable diseases are available.

Part II

In this part of the test each item consists of an underlined incomplete sentence, with several given endings. Place a T in the blank before each ending which makes the completed sentence true, and an O before each ending which makes the completed sentence false.

A. Some bacilli have flagella

   ___T___ 61. entirely absent

   ___O___ 62. on their top surface only

   ___T___ 63. over the entire surface of the cell

   ___O___ 64. on the bottom surface only

   ___T___ 65. at one end of the cell

   ___T___ 66. at both ends of the cell

B. In Millburn, quarantine is imposed upon persons exposed to

   ___T___ 67. diphtheria

   ___O___ 68. colds

   ___O___ 69. malaria

   ___T___ 70. mumps

   ___T___ 71. scarlet fever

   ___O___ 72. syphilis

   ___O___ 73. typhoid fever

C. One of the available "3 cents a day" hospitalization plans pays for hospital services including

   ___O___ 74. operating fees of surgeons

   ___T___ 75. maternal services eleven months or longer after entering plan

   ___O___ 76. treatment of mental diseases

   ___T___ 77. use of the operating room

   ___T___ 78. giving the anaesthetic by an employee of the hospital

   ___T___ 79. treatment of diseases by X-rays

D. It is possible effectively to immunize persons against

   ___T___ 80. chicken pox

   ___O___ 81. gonorrhea

___O___ 82. influenza

___T___ 83. measles

___O___ 84. pneumonia

___T___ 85. smallpox

___O___ 86. tuberculosis

___O___ 87. whooping cough

E. Some of the common symptoms of communicable diseases are

___T___ 88. fever

___O___ 89. prolonged gain in weight

___T___ 90. skin rash

___T___ 91. sore throat

___O___ 92. constipation

___T___ 93. aching joints

F. Communicable diseases may be spread by means of

___T___ 94. contaminated foods

___T___ 95. articles soiled by discharges from respiratory systems of ill persons

___T___ 96. insects

___O___ 97. swamp ˑˑ

___O___ 98. contaminated water

___O___ 99. wild song birds

PART III

The items in this part of the test consist of incomplete sentences with several suggested endings. One, and only one, ending will make the completed statement true. Place the letter of the one true ending in the blank before the incomplete statement.

___B___ 100. Milk is pasteurized by being heated for thirty minutes at a temperature of a. 40° F.; b. 140° F.; c. 212° F.; d. 500° F.; e. 2000° F.

___A___ 101. The number of cases of smallpox in this nation during the past twenty years has shown a. a general decrease; b. a general increase; c. little change from year to year; d. that the disease has been totally eliminated; e. that we are due for a great epidemic next year

___E___ 102. The number of deaths due to influenza in 1929 was reported at a. 800,000; b. 220,000; c. 150,000; d. 92,000; e. 66,000

___C___ 103. The annual number of deaths due to tuberculosis in this nation is about a. 750; b. 2,500; c. 75,000; d. 200,000; e. 500,000

___C___ 104. An injection of diphtheria toxin is given a child to determine if he can contract diphtheria. If he *can* contract it, the skin at the place of injection will a. show no reaction;

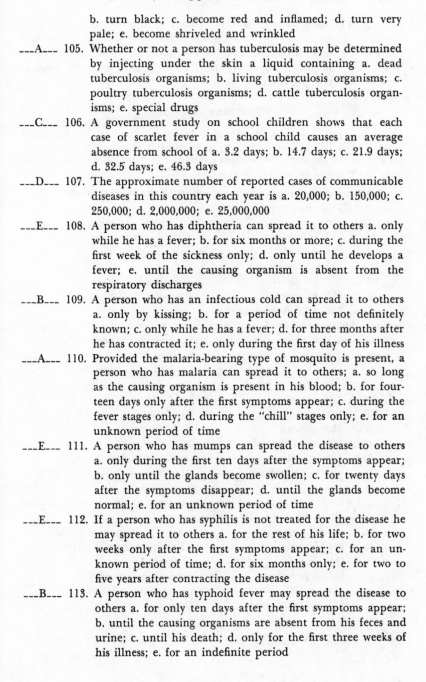

b. turn black; c. become red and inflamed; d. turn very pale; e. become shriveled and wrinkled

___A___ 105. Whether or not a person has tuberculosis may be determined by injecting under the skin a liquid containing a. dead tuberculosis organisms; b. living tuberculosis organisms; c. poultry tuberculosis organisms; d. cattle tuberculosis organisms; e. special drugs

___C___ 106. A government study on school children shows that each case of scarlet fever in a school child causes an average absence from school of a. 3.2 days; b. 14.7 days; c. 21.9 days; d. 32.5 days; e. 46.3 days

___D___ 107. The approximate number of reported cases of communicable diseases in this country each year is a. 20,000; b. 150,000; c. 250,000; d. 2,000,000; e. 25,000,000

___E___ 108. A person who has diphtheria can spread it to others a. only while he has a fever; b. for six months or more; c. during the first week of the sickness only; d. only until he develops a fever; e. until the causing organism is absent from the respiratory discharges

___B___ 109. A person who has an infectious cold can spread it to others a. only by kissing; b. for a period of time not definitely known; c. only while he has a fever; d. for three months after he has contracted it; e. only during the first day of his illness

___A___ 110. Provided the malaria-bearing type of mosquito is present, a person who has malaria can spread it to others; a. so long as the causing organism is present in his blood; b. for fourteen days only after the first symptoms appear; c. during the fever stages only; d. during the "chill" stages only; e. for an unknown period of time

___E___ 111. A person who has mumps can spread the disease to others a. only during the first ten days after the symptoms appear; b. only until the glands become swollen; c. for twenty days after the symptoms disappear; d. until the glands become normal; e. for an unknown period of time

___E___ 112. If a person who has syphilis is not treated for the disease he may spread it to others a. for the rest of his life; b. for two weeks only after the first symptoms appear; c. for an unknown period of time; d. for six months only; e. for two to five years after contracting the disease

___B___ 113. A person who has typhoid fever may spread the disease to others a. for only ten days after the first symptoms appear; b. until the causing organisms are absent from his feces and urine; c. until his death; d. only for the first three weeks of his illness; e. for an indefinite period

___A___ 114. Silver nitrate solution is used in the eyes of newly born infants to prevent blindness resulting from a. gonorrheal infection at birth; b. injuries suffered during birth; c. premature birth; d. syphilis infection at birth; e. infection by bacteria from the air

PART IV

In this part of the test you are to match the proper terms in the right-hand column with the corresponding term in the left column. You may not need to use all the items in the right column. Place the letter of the correct term in the blank before the item on the left.

A. Match the disease-producing organisms with the listed diseases.

___A___	115. chicken pox	
___D___	116. gonorrhea	Causing organisms
___A___	117. influenza	a. filtrable virus
___A___	118. measles	b. spirochete
___D___	119. pneumonia	c. rod bacteria
___A___	120. smallpox	d. spherical bacteria
___C___	121. tuberculosis	e. Protozoa
___C___	122. whooping cough	

B. Each disease has a period of incubation, which is the time from exposure to the disease until the first symptoms appear. Match the periods of incubation with the diseases listed.

		Periods of incubation
___E___	123. diphtheria	a. 1 to 3 days
___A___	124. colds	b. 1 to 30 days
___F___	125. malaria	c. 2 to 7 days
___G___	126. mumps	d. 10 to 42 days
___C___	127. scarlet fever	e. 2 to 5 days
___D___	128. syphilis	f. usually to 14 days
___H___	129. typhoid fever	g. 12 to 26 days
		h. 3 to 38 days

C. Match with each disease the kind of immunity, if any, one may acquire as the result of having had the disease.

___C___	130. diphtheria	Kind of Immunity Usually
___A___	131. malaria	Resulting from the Disease
___B___	132. mumps	a. no immunity
___C___	133. scarlet fever	b. temporary immunity
___A___	134. syphilis	c. permanent immunity
___C___	135. typhoid fever	d. inherited immunity

D. Match the diseases listed with the age groups in which these diseases occur, as listed on the right.

---A--- 136. diphtheria

---D--- 137. malaria

---A--- 138. mumps

---A--- 139. scarlet fever

---D--- 140. syphilis

---D--- 141. typhoid fever

Age Groups

a. children most often

b. very old people only

c. adults only

d. both adults and children

E. The place from which disease germs are spread is called the source of infection. Match the sources of infection with the diseases listed.

---B--- 142. chicken pox

---C--- 143. gonorrhea

---A--- 144. influenza

---A--- 145. pneumonia

---A--- 146. tuberculosis

---A--- 147. whooping cough.

Sources of Infection

a. discharges from respiratory system

b. scabs or crusts on skin

c. discharges from sores on reproductive organs

d. healthy carriers

F. Match the terms on the left with the definitions which fit them best.

---C--- 148. lysin

--- B --- 149. agglutinin

---D--- 150. antitoxin

Definitions

a. a substance produced by disease bacteria

b. a substance which causes bacteria to be clumped together

c. a substance which dissolves bacteria

d. a substance formed by the body to help it fight diseases

FORM B

Name _____ Grade _____ Home Room _____ Class _____

Some of the following statements are true and some are false. Mark the true statements with a T, and the false statements with an O.

___O___ 1. Cells of filtrable viruses may be seen with an optical microscope.

___T___ 2. Inclusion bodies are found in cells infected with smallpox.

___O___ 3. Malaria may be controlled by the extermination of ticks.

___O___ 4. The Dick test shows whether one can contract parrot fever.

___O___ 5. Typhoid vaccination is done by scratching the skin with a needle containing the vaccine.

___T___ 6. The existence of filterable viruses can be proved experimentally.

___T___ 7. True disinfectants are substances which kill bacteria.

___T___ 8. Bacteria spores can survive conditions unfavorable to bacteria in the vegetative form.

___T___ 9. Fibrin is removed from the blood from which diphtheria antitoxin is prepared.

___T___ 10. The Wassermann test helps to determine whether a person has syphilis.

___O___ 11. Passive immunity is ordinarily more lasting than active immunity.

___O___ 12. Koch developed vaccination against smallpox.

___T___ 13. Semmelweiss discovered that the use of antiseptics helps to prevent childbirth fever.

___O___ 14. Filterable viruses are large carbohydrate molecules.

___T___ 15. Ehrlich developed a chemical cure for syphilis.

___T___ 16. Oysters from contaminated water may spread typhoid fever.

___O___ 17. Resistance to diseases is high in persons who are in poor physical condition.

___O___ 18. Malaria is more common in northern than in southern states.

___T___ 19. Rabies is caused by a filterable virus.

___O___ 20. One species of bacterium may cause several different diseases.

___T___ 21. Araphenamine is a drug used in the treatment of syphilis.

___T___ 22. Rat fleas spread bubonic plague.

___T___ 23. Smallpox cases increase in number when compulsory vaccination laws are repealed.

___O___ 24. Sulfanilamide compounds are especially effective against the rod bacteria.

___O___ 25. Malaria is transmitted to man by the Culex mosquito.

___T___ 26. Typhoid vaccine contains large numbers of dead typhoid germs.

---T--- 27. Horses are a source of infection for one type of sleeping sickness.

---O--- 28. Leprosy is a common disease in the continental United States.

---O--- 29. Cases of bubonic plague have never occurred in the United States.

---T--- 30. Athlete's foot is a communicable disease.

---T--- 31. Some communicable diseases are due to the poisons produced by bacteria in the body.

---O--- 32. Typhoid fever is most prevalent in large cities.

---T--- 33. Yellow fever is caused by a filterable virus.

---T--- 34. Germicides are substances which kill germs.

---T--- 35. Fleas on ground squirrels may transmit bubonc plague.

---T--- 36. Spirochetes have a corkscrew shape.

---O--- 37. Smallpox vaccine is obtained from sheep.

---O--- 38. The Schick test shows whether a person can contract mumps.

---O--- 39. Spirochetes are many-celled organisms.

---O--- 40. Malaria organisms destroy white blood corpuscles in man.

---O--- 41. Modern medical practice recommends that a shield be worn over a newly made smallpox vaccination.

---T--- 42. The babies of mothers suffering from syphilis are often born dead.

---O--- 43. Tuberculosis is now one of the rarest diseases in the United States.

---O--- 44. Toxoids are altered toxins having more poisonous effects.

---O--- 45. Prevention of diseases is less important than curing them.

---O--- 46. That diseases may be communicable was not discovered until 1920.

---O--- 47. The normal temperature of the human body is unfavorable to the development of germs in it.

---O--- 48. It is safe to prescribe medicines for one's self when one has a light case of a communicable disease.

---T--- 49. The period of recovery from a disease is called convalescence.

---O--- 50. Communicable diseases are frequently spread through use of canned foods.

---O--- 51. Cowpox is a form of measles in cattle.

---T--- 52. Disease organisms may be carried to the mouth by unclean hands.

---T--- 53. Water of doubtful bacteriological purity may be made safe for drinking by boiling it.

---O--- 54. Chlorination makes water unsafe for drinking.

---T--- 55. Rocky Mountain spotted fever has been reported from all major areas of the United States.

---T--- 56. Most species of bacteria are harmless to man.

---O--- 57. Bacteria can manufacture their own food.

___O___ 58. Cancer is generally believed to be caused by germs.

___O___ 59. Negroes are less susceptible to tuberculosis than white persons.

___T___ 60. A "healthy carrier" is one who carries the germs of a disease in his body without suffering from the disease.

PART II

In this part of the test each item consists of an underlined incomplete sentence, with several given endings. Place a T in the blank before each ending which makes the completed sentence true, and an O before each ending which makes the completed sentence false.

A. Millburn health regulations require quarantine for persons exposed to

   ___O___ 61. gonorrhea

   ___O___ 62. influenza

   ___T___ 63. measles

   ___O___ 64. pneumonia

   ___T___ 65. smallpox

   ___O___ 66. tuberculosis

   ___T___ 67. whooping cough

B. The Millburn Board of Health is legally responsible for

   ___T___ 68. regulating sanitation in places where food is sold

   ___T___ 69. setting up standards for the milk supply

   ___O___ 70. inspecting homes to see that they are kept clean

   ___O___ 71. inspecting public buildings for fire hazards

   ___O___ 72. maintaining cleanliness in the public schools

   ___T___ 73. proper disposal of garbage

   ___T___ 74. proper disposal of sewage

C. One of the available "3 cents a day" hospitalization plans pays for services including

   ___O___ 75. bed and board in a private room for twenty-one days

   ___O___ 76. treatment of diseases requiring isolation

   ___T___ 77. general nursing service

   ___O___ 78. treatment of diseases contracted before entering the plan

   ___O___ 79. blood transfusions

   ___T___ 80. use of X-rays for determining what diseases the patient has

D. It is possible effectively to immunize persons against

   ___T___ 81. diphtheria

   ___O___ 82. infantile paralysis

   ___O___ 83. malaria

   ___O___ 84. mumps

   ___O___ 85. scarlet fever

   ___O___ 86. syphilis

   ___O___ 87. typhoid fever

E. Some of the common symptoms of communicable diseases are

---T--- 88. coughing
---O--- 89. nose bleeding
---T--- 90. "running" nose
---T--- 91. chills
---T--- 92. headache
---O--- 93. decaying teeth

F. Communicable diseases may be spread by means of

---T--- 94. contact with articles soiled by body discharges of sick person
---O--- 95. preserved foods
---T--- 96. healthy carriers
---O--- 97. clothes washed in public laundries
---T--- 98. kissing the person who is ill
---T--- 99. droplets from the mouth of sick persons

Part III

The items in this part of the test consist of incomplete sentences with several suggested endings. One, and only one, ending will make the completed statement true. Place the letter of the one true ending in the blank before the incomplete statement.

---E--- 100. The number of bacteria which would weigh one gram has been estimated at a. 500; b. 20,000; c. 1,000,000; d. 7,500,000; e. 500,000,000,000

---A--- 101. In each spore formation, a bacterium produces a. 1 spore; b. 3 spores; c. 6 spores; d. 15 spores; e. 100 spores

---E--- 102. The number of cases of scarlet fever reported in the nation in 1935 was a. 150; b. 2,700; c. 18,000; d. 60,000; e. 95,000

---C--- 103. The number of persons who die of pneumonia each year in this country is about a. 2,000; b. 49,000; c. 100,000; d. 450,000; e. 1,000,000

---A--- 104. An injection of diluted scarlet fever toxin is given a child to determine whether or not he can contract the disease. If he *can* contract it, the skin at the point of injection will a. become inflamed and red; b. turn black and blue; c. peel off in large flakes; d. remain normal; e. become wrinkled and dry.

---A--- 105. Active acquired immunity results from a. formation of antibodies by the body itself; b. increase in the number of red corpuscles; c. formation of fibrin from fibrinogen; d. diseases suffered three times; e. injection of antibodies produced in an animal

---B--- 106. Antitoxins formed to counteract one disease are effective against a. all communicable diseases; b. the disease which

caused their formation; c. all diseases caused by bacteria;
d. the disease contracted next; e. degenerative diseases

___D___ 107. A person who has chicken pox may spread the disease to others a. during the remainder of his life; b. one to three days after his rash appears; c. three to six weeks after his rash appears; d. six to ten days after his rash appears; e. for an unknown period of time

___E___ 108. A person with gonorrhea may spread the disease to others a. until all gonorrhea sores on his body heal; b. during the rest of his life if he is not treated; c. for only two months after he is infected; d. for two years after he is infected; e. so long as the causing organisms are present in any of his body discharges

___A___ 109. A person who has influenza may spread it to others a. for an unknown period of time; b. for fourteen days after his first symptoms appear; c. only while he has a fever; d. for seven days after he has recovered; e. only one day after becoming ill

___B___ 110. A person who has measles may spread the disease to others a. only while he is recovering; b. during the period of excessive discharge from nose and throat; c. for three weeks after the appearance of the rash; d. for eight to ten days after his recovery; e. for twelve to fourteen days before his recovery

___C___ 111. A person who has pneumonia may spread the disease to others a. so long as he has a fever; b. for one to three days; c. for an unknown period of time; d. until he dies; e. for two weeks after he becomes ill

___A___ 112. A person who has smallpox may spread it to others a. until all crusts and scabs disappear; b. until he is immunized; c. only while he has a fever; d. for ten days only after the symptoms appear; e. for two weeks after he becomes ill

___D___ 113. A person who has tuberculosis may spread the disease to others a. until he dies; b. so long as the causing organisms are in his body; c. for two years after he becomes infected; d. so long as he is eliminating the causing organism from his body; e. for only two weeks after he is first infected

___C___ 114. A government study on school children shows that each case of whooping cough in a school child causes an average absence from school of a. 3 days; b. 10 days; c. 26 days; d. 35 days; e. 43 days

Part IV

In this part of the test you are to match the proper terms in the right-hand column with the corresponding terms in the left column. You may not need to use all the items in the right column. Place the letter of the correct term in the blank before the items on the left.

A. Match the disease-producing organisms with the listed diseases.

___C___ 115. diphtheria   Causing Organism

___B___ 116. colds   a. spore Protozoa

___A___ 117. malaria   b. filterable virus

___B___ 118. mumps   c. rod bacteria

___E___ 119. scarlet fever   d. flagellated Protozoa

___F___ 120. syphilis   e. spherical bacteria

___C___ 121. typhoid fever   f. Spirochete

B. Each disease has a period of incubation which is the time from exposure to the disease until the first symptoms appear. Match the periods of incubation with the diseases listed.

___E___ 122. chicken pox   Periods of Incubation

___D___ 123. gonorrhea   a. 1 to 3 days

___A___ 124. influenza   b. 2 to 20 days

___H___ 125. measles   c. 7, not more than 16 days

___A___ 126. pneumonia   d. 1 to 8 days

___F___ 127. smallpox   e. 14 to 21 days

___G___ 128. tuberculosis   f. 8 to 16 days

___C___ 129. whooping cough   g. extremely variable

     h. 8 to 14 days

C. Match with each disease the kind of immunity, if any, one may acquire as the result of having had the disease.

___A___ 130. gonorrhea   Kind of Immunity Usually

___B___ 131. influenza   Resulting from the Disease

___B___ 132. pneumonia   a. no immunity

___A___ 133. tuberculosis   b. temporary immunity

___D___ 134. whooping cough   c. inherited immunity

___D___ 135. measles   d. permanent immunity

D. Match the diseases listed with the age groups in which they occur most frequently.

___A___ 136. chicken pox

___D___ 137. gonorrhea   Age Groups

___A___ 138. measles   a. children most often

___D___ 139. pneumonia   b. very old people only

___D___ 140. smallpox   c. adults only

___D___ 141. tuberculosis   d. both adults and children

E. The place from which disease germs are spread is called the source of infection. Match the sources of infection with the diseases listed.

Sources of Infection

___A___ 142. diphtheria

___A___ 143. colds

___A___ 144. mumps

___A___ 145. scarlet fever

___E___ 146. syphilis

___B___ 147. typhoid fever

a. discharges from the respiratory system

b. bowel discharges or urine

c. rashes or sores on skin

d. blood of an infected person

e. sores on reproductive organs

F. Match the terms on the left with the definitions which fit them best.

Definitions

a. a substance which aids white corpuscles in digesting bacteria

b. a substance which causes bacteria to clump together and settle to the bottom of a test tube

___A___ 148. opsonin

___C___ 149. toxin

___D___ 150. antibody

c. a poisonous substance secreted by disease bacteria

d. a substance produced by the body to fight disease organisms

VITA

JOHN URBAN, born, June 1, 1909, at Tisovec, Austria-Hungary (Slovakia).

Educational Institutions Attended: Cleveland, Ohio, Public Grammar Schools, 1915–1921. Brimfield, Ohio, Public School, 1921–1925. Kent, Ohio, Roosevelt High School, Graduated 1926. Kent State University, 1927–1930; B.S. in Education, 1930. Marine Biological Laboratory, Woods Hole, Mass, Summer, 1933. Teachers College, Columbia University, Summer 1934, 1935; A.M., August, 1935. Columbia University, 1935–1936. Teachers College, Columbia University, 1935–1936; Summers 1936, 1937, 1938, 1939, 1941; also 1936–1937, 1938–1939.

Previous Publication: "Understanding Pneumonia," in collaboration with James A. Brill and Dale C. Stahl, M.D. Erpi Classroom Films, Inc., 35—11 Thirty-fifth Avenue, Long Island City, New York, 1941.